A Graphics Toolkit

I0487265

Randi J. Rost

Produced by:
Brian Wiser & Bill Martens

 Apple PugetSound Program Library Exchange

A Graphics Toolkit

Copyright © 1984-1986, 2022 by Apple Pugetsound Program Library Exchange (A.P.P.L.E.) All Rights Reserved. www.callapple.org

Paperback ISBN: 978-1-387-82204-1
Hardback ISBN: 978-1-387-81952-2

ACKNOWLEDGEMENTS

A Graphics Toolkit was created by Randi J. Rost in 1984. This A.P.P.L.E. book is an excerpt of our sixth In Depth series book, *All About Graphics*. It is based on "A Graphics Toolkit" articles from *Call-A.P.P.L.E.* magazine over three years found in these issues: 1984 (April, May, August, December), 1985 (June, December), and 1986 (January, November, December).

PRODUCTION

Brian Wiser → Design, Layout, Editing, Cover
Bill Martens → Original Layout, Code Extractions, Disk Creation

DISCLAIMER

No part of this manual may be reproduced, distributed or transmitted in any form or by any means, including photocopying, recording, or other electronic or mechanical methods, without prior written permission of the publisher, except in the case of brief quotations contained in articles and reviews, and program listings which may be entered, stored and executed in a computer system, but not reproduced for publication.

A Graphics Toolkit disk image is available from the publisher's site: www.callapple.org. No warranty of disk images or programs is made or implied and should be used at your own risk.

A Graphics Toolkit is an independent publication and has not been authorized, sponsored, or otherwise approved by any institution, public or private. All images are under copyright and the property of Apple Pugetsound Program Library Exchange, or as otherwise indicated. Use is prohibited without prior permission.

Apple and all Apple hardware and software brand names are trademarks of Apple Inc., registered in the United States and other countries. All other brand names and trademarks are the property of their respective owners.

While all possible steps have been taken to ensure that the information included within is accurate, the publisher, producers, and authors shall have no liability or responsibility for any errors or omissions, or for loss or damages resulting from the use of the information and programs contained herein.

About Randi J. Rost

Randi J. Rost works at Intel where he has held a variety of roles in developer relations over 15 years, including leading the Intel game developer program for five years.

He majored in computer science at Minnesota State, Mankato and he received a Master's Degree in Computing Science with an emphasis in computer graphics from the University of California, Davis.

While still an undergrad, Randi purchased an Apple II computer, and wrote and published a game called *King Cribbage*. A *Graphics Toolkit* was intended to be the heart of a new game, but this project proved to be too much with graduate studies and his first job, so Randi turned it into a series of instructional articles instead.

Randi lives in Loveland, Colorado with his wife, Teresa.

About the Producers

Brian Wiser

Brian Wiser is a producer of books, films, games, and events, as well as a long-time consultant, enthusiast and historian of Apple, the Apple II and Macintosh. Steve Wozniak and Steve Jobs, as well as *Creative Computing*, *Nibble*, *InCider*, and *A+* magazines were early influences.

Brian designed, edited, and co-produced dozens of books including: *Nibble Viewpoints: Business Insights From The Computing Revolution*, *Cyber Jack: The Adventures of Robert Clardy and Synergistic Software*, *Synergistic Software: The Early Games*, *The Colossal Computer Cartoon Book: Enhanced Edition*, *All About Applesoft: Enhanced Edition*, *Graphically Speaking: Enhanced Edition*, *What's Where in the Apple: Enhanced Edition*, and *The WOZPAK: Special Edition* – an important Apple II historical book with Steve Wozniak's restored original, technical handwritten notes. Brian is also the author of *The Etch-a-Sketch and Other Fun Programs*.

He passionately preserves and archives all facets of Apple's history, and noteworthy companies such as Beagle Bros and Applied Engineering, featured on AppleArchives.com. His writing, interviews and books are featured on the technology news site CallApple.org and in *Call-A.P.P.L.E.* magazine that he co-produces as an A.P.P.L.E. board member. Brian also co-produced the retro iOS game *Structris*.

In 2005, Brian was cast as an extra in Joss Whedon's movie *Serenity*, leading him to being a producer and director for the documentary film *Done The Impossible: The Fans' Tale of Firefly & Serenity*. He brought some of the *Firefly* cast aboard his Browncoat Cruise and recruited several of the *Firefly* cast to appear in a film for charity. Throughout these experiences, he develops close personal relationships with many actors, authors, and computer industry luminaries. Brian speaks about his adventures to large audiences at conventions around the country.

Bill Martens

Bill Martens is a systems engineer specializing in office infrastructures and has been programming since 1976. The DEC PDP 11/40 with ASR-33 Teletypes and CRT's were his first computing platforms with his first forays in the Apple world coming with the Apple II computer.

Influences in Bill's computing life came from *Byte* magazine, *Creative Computing* magazine, and *Call-A.P.P.L.E.* magazine as well as his mentors Samuel Perkins, Don Williams, Joff Morgan, and Mike Christensen.

Bill is the author of *ApPilot/W1*, *Beyond Quest*, *The Anatomy of an EAMON*, and multiple EAMon adventure games, as well as a co-producer of many books including *What's Where in the Apple: Enhanced Edition*, *The WOZPAK: Special Edition*, *Nibble Viewpoints: Business Insights From The Computing Revolution*, and co-programmer for the iOS version of the retro game *Structris*. He has written many articles which have appeared in user group newsletters and magazines such as Call-A.P.P.L.E..

Bill worked for Apple Pugetsound Program Library Exchange (A.P.P.L.E.) under Val Golding and Dick Hubert as a data manager and programmer in the 1980s, and is the current president of the A.P.P.L.E. user group established in 1978. He reorganized A.P.P.L.E. and restarted *Call-A.P.P.L.E.* magazine in 2002. He is the production editor for the A.P.P.L.E. website CallApple.org, writes science fiction novels in his spare time, and is a retired semi-pro football player.

CONTENTS

CHAPTER 4   35

CHAPTER 5   43

CHAPTER 1

Hello everyone, and welcome to the first chapter of *A Graphics Toolkit.* If all of you dutifully type in the program listings, or download the disk image from www.callapple.org, you'll soon have a useful library of machine language graphics routines that you can draw upon for all sorts of applications. Bear with me as I get some philosophical introductory remarks out of the way.

I. Introduction

Stating the problem to be solved before actually going ahead and solving the problem always helps to focus one's thinking. This is referred to, logically enough, as the problem statement. What is the goal of this series? The main goal is to share some machine language routines that will be useful for graphics applications such as animation and games. Along the way, I hope to explain a few of the intricacies of graphics on the Apple II as well as discuss some general graphics algorithms. During the course of this series, we'll be developing routines to draw lines, plot block shapes, and all sorts of wonderful things. I'll also take time out every so often to encourage some progressive thinking on software engineering. Those who take my words to heart will only be ahead of the game when it comes to producing 1980s-style software.

What will you need in order to get something out of this series? An assembler is necessary for those of you who wish to use the routines that will be presented. I recommend the *Big Mac* assembler from A.P.P.L.E., not because it's from A.P.P.L.E., but because it's the best. It also happens to be a steal if you're an A.P.P.L.E. member.

I will be presuming some knowledge of 6502 machine language and of graphics on the Apple in general. The routines presented will either be assembly language or Applesoft. If you have any qualms about any of this, don't worry just yet. Everyone should go back and review Loy Spurlock's excellent article "Understanding High-Res Graphics" in the January 1980 issue of *Call-A.P.P.L.E.* or the 1980 anthology volume.

1

Many other recent articles can provide some general information on Apple graphics. These include Mark Pelczarski's *Graphically Speaking: Enhanced Edition* book, Roger Wagner's "Assembly Lines" in past issues of *Softalk*, David Lubar's series "The Graph Paper" in *Creative Computing,* and Ken Williams treatment of the topic in *Softline.*

II. Tools and Toolkits

What is a tool? A tool is something that is used by a craftsperson or a laborer to make their work easier. To call something a tool also often implies reusability, that is, the tool can be used every time the circumstances warrant its use. A toolkit in the software sense then might simply be a collection of subroutines that can simplify a specific programming task. In this case, we have chosen graphics as our applications area. Reusability implies that this collection of routines will be well documented and easy enough to use so that it can be picked up a year later and still be useable.

There were five major goals established in the development of the routines that will appear in this series. I'll list them in the order in which they influenced the design of the overall package and leave it up to you to see how well the goals were met. The goals were:

1. Flexibility/Generality
2. Speed
3. Ease of use
4. Modularity
5. Compactness

Surprised to see speed ranked number two? Actually the first three were all very close in terms of importance, and the last two were somewhat more secondary considerations. These routines all stemmed out of a desire to develop the tools necessary to write an arcade-quality game on the Apple II. At the same time, there was a strong desire to make the routines as easy to use as possible so that friends and relatives with Apples could use them as well.
Feel free to use these routines in any of your own programs.

III. Apple Graphics

Ok, let's get to the heart of the matter. You will recall that the primary High-Res page lives in the memory range $2000-$3FFF (all numbers preceded by dollar signs are in hexadecimal) and High-Res page two resides in range $4000-$5FFF. Each row of 280 pixels on the High-Res screen corresponds to a 40 byte sequence in memory. The address of the first byte in the sequence depends on the y-value, or row number, and whether the row is part of High-Res page 1 or High-Res page 2.

Unfortunately, the rows of the High-Res screen are not mapped sequentially into the High-Res memory area, but in a somewhat complicated non-sequential pattern. This pattern is visible whenever you type the Applesoft command "HGR" to clear a cluttered graphics screen. The screen is not cleared in order from top to bottom but appears to be divided into bands of about eight lines each that are erased simultaneously. In fact, the value for black is being loaded sequentially into every location from $2000-$3FFF and the effect you are seeing demonstrates that any given row on the screen does not immediately precede in the memory scheme the row directly beneath it on the screen.

Spurlock derived a formula for calculating the address of the first byte of row given only its row number (y-value) in the *Call-A.P.P.L.E.* article mentioned earlier. More on this topic a little later.

Once you have found the address of the first byte in the row, the rest is a little easier. Since there are 280 pixels in a row and 40 bytes in which to store the on/off information for one row, it seems reasonable that each byte will contain on/off information for seven pixels. This is exactly what happens. The eighth bit in each byte, the most significant bit, is used as a color flag for the seven pixels in the byte.

The pattern contained in a specific byte determines the color and on/off information for seven pixels on the screen. If all seven pixel bits are zeros, (off) then we have black in those seven pixels on the screen. Since the color bit may be either one or zero, we have two ways of representing black. The same is true for white. All seven pixel bits can be ones (on) to display a short white line on the screen, and the color bit can be either on or off, giving us two ways to create white.

Colors are formed in a similar manner. It turns out that alternating pixels in an on-off-on-off pattern will cause a color other than white or black to be created. Since the pattern can be either on-off-on-etc. or off-on-off-etc. and the color bit can be either on or off, we have four more colors (violet, green, orange, and blue) that may be used. Since it takes an on-off pair to make a dot on the screen in one of these colors, the resolution of the High-Res screen is really only 140x192 for colors other than white and black. This also means that vertical lines in these colors will cause problems. Green and orange vertical lines can be seen in odd columns but not in even columns, and for blue and violet the opposite is true.

Allowing the color flag to control the color of seven pixels causes another well-known problem: "unexpected" color changes when drawing lines or shapes using a color whose the color flag is different than the color flag of the background. The new pixel is plotted as one of the seven on/off bits in the byte, and the color flag is changed.

The result is that the other six bits in the byte now have a different color flag than before and may be displayed as a completely different color. There really is no solution to this problem, other than precluding the problem a priori by choosing background and foreground colors that do not interfere in such a manner.

Listing 1.1 — Toolkit Initialization

```
100  REM  -- INITIALIZATION --
110 A = 8192
200  REM  -- POKE Y-HI VALUES --
210  FOR I = 1 TO 3
220 :: FOR J = 0 TO 3
230 :::: FOR K = 1 TO 2
240 :::::: FOR L = J TO J + 28 STEP 4
250 :::::::: POKE A,L
260 ::::::::A = A + 1
270  NEXT L,K,J,I
300  REM  -- POKE Y-LO VALUES --
310  FOR I = 1 TO 3
320 :: READ YLO(1),YLO(2)
330 :: FOR J = 1 TO 4
340 :::: FOR K = 1 TO 2
350 :::::: FOR L = 1 TO 8
360 :::::::: POKE A,YLO(K)
370 ::::::::A = A + 1
380  NEXT L,K,J,I
390  DATA  0,128,40,168,80,208
400  REM  -- POKE COLOR MASK TABLE --
410  FOR I = 1 TO 8
420 :: READ COLMASK
430 :: POKE A,COLMASK
440 ::A = A + 1
450  NEXT I
460  DATA  0,42,85,127,128,170,213,255
500  REM  -- POKE BIT POSITION TABLE --
510  FOR I = 0 TO 6
520 :: POKE A,128 + 2 ^ I
530 ::A = A + 1
540  NEXT I
600  REM  -- POKE X/7 TABLE --
610  FOR I = 0 TO 57
620 :: FOR J = 1 TO 7
630 :::: POKE A,I
640 ::::A = A + 1
650  NEXT J,I
700  REM  -- POKE (X MOD 7) + 1 TABLE --
710  FOR I = 0 TO 57
720 :: FOR J = 1 TO 7
730 :::: POKE A,J
```

```
740 ::::A = A + 1
750  NEXT J,I
800  REM  -- CHECK FOR ACCURACY --
810 SUM = 0
820  FOR I = 8192 TO A - 1
830 ::SUM = SUM +  PEEK (I)
840 :: IF SUM > 255 THEN SUM = SUM - 255
850  NEXT I
855  TEXT : HOME : VTAB 8
860  PRINT "CHECKSUM IS -- ";SUM
870  PRINT
880  IF SUM < > 187 THEN  PRINT "ERROR -- CHECKSUM SHOULD
EQUAL 187.": PRINT "PLEASE RECHECK YOUR PROGRAM.": GOTO 1000
900  PRINT  CHR$ (4);"BSAVE YTABLE,A$2000,L$4BB"
1000  END
```

IV. Lookups

What is the fastest way to multiply two numbers together on a computer? Before you start describing efficient multiplication algorithms, think a little harder. On nearly any computer, the fastest way to multiply two numbers is to use a large table to store all the answers, and use the two numbers as indices into the table. Once the proper location in the table is found, it's simply a matter of reading the answer. This method is commonly referred to as "table look-up." The sheer size of this table for multiplication of two arbitrary numbers makes it infeasible in this case, but it can be used to great advantage in speeding up calculations if the table does not have to be very large.

The address of the first byte in any particular row of the High-Res screen can be calculated given only the row number, but it turns out that a 20-30 line machine language routine is needed. Since there are only 192 rows on the High-Res screen, it appears we can save a good deal of calculation with a table that's not too large. In this case we need two 192byte tables, one for the high byte of the address and one for the low byte. Doing two indexed memory accesses will give us the address of any row. This will speed up the row address calculation by more than a factor of 20!

Listing 1 contains an Applesoft program that will POKE into memory all the tables that will be used by all the graphics routines to be presented in this series. The first table contains the high byte base address for each of the 192 rows. Adding $20 to this value will result in an address on High-Res page one, and adding $40 yields an address on page two. The second table contains the low byte of the base address for the row.

Following these two tables are two very short tables. The first is called the color mask table and contains eight bytes, one for each of the eight possible High-Res colors. Each byte in this table contains the bit pattern (on-off-on...or whatever) that is needed to render that particular color on the display. Following that is a seven-byte table called the bit-position table. Each byte in this table contains a one in the color flag bit and a one in the bit which corresponds to its location within the table. For instance the first entry has bit zero set, the second entry has bit one set, etc.

The fifth and sixth tables also speed up computations. They contain values for locating the specific byte within a row and the bit within that byte for a specific x-coordinate on the screen. The fifth table contains values of x/7 since dividing by seven is a time-consuming operation compared to a table lookup. The sixth table contains values for (x mod 7) + 1, and we'll see how those values will be useful later on in the series.

The program in Listing 1.1 will try to do a checksum on the POKEd values, and if the result is successful, it will save the tables onto your disk under the name YTABLE. As you can see, this file contains only data values and so is completely relocatable. It can be loaded into memory anywhere there is enough space, and is just over 1K bytes long.

V. Initialization

In just about any programming task, there are a few activities that must be carried out under the heading of initialization, and this is no exception. We have created a set of lookup tables that are completely relocatable, but our other routines will need to know where those tables have been loaded. The initialization routine in Listing 2 will take care of installing the necessary pointers to our lookup tables.

The initialization routine should be called with the address of the YTABLE in the A and X-registers. Right from the start let's adopt the convention that whenever it's necessary to pass an address to a

7

routine, it will be passed with the high byte of the address in the A-register and the low byte in X. This will keep address-passing consistent and easy to remember for all of our routines. In this case, if our YTABLE was loaded at $1000, the first thing we'd need in our program is a JSR INIT after loading the A register with a $10 and the X-register with zero. The INIT routine will then set up the necessary pointers so that later routines will know where to find the lookup tables.

Later on in the series we'll be adding a couple more things to the initialization routine.

Listing 1.2 - Hi-Res Graphics Subroutines

```
AST 32
*                                    *
*  HI-RES GRAPHICS SUBROUTINES *
*                                    *
*      by  Randi J. Rost        *
*                                    *
* Call -A.P.P.L.E. : Apr. 1984 *
*      All rights reserved      *
*                                    *
  AST 32
*
*
*
* The INIT subroutine should be called with
*  the lo byte of the YTABLE address in X and
*  the hi byte in A.  Other ptrs are then installed.
*
*
  ORG $803
YTABL = $EC
YTABH = $EE
POSTABL = $4A
XDIVTBL = $4C
XMODTBL = $D0
COLTABL = $FE
INIT STA YTABH+1
```

```
STX YTABH
TXA
CLC
ADC #$C0 ;Get starting loc for
STA YTABL ;Y-lo values table
LDA #$00

ADC YTABH+1
STA YTABL+1
CLC
LDA YTABL
ADC #$C0 ;Get starting loc for
STA COLTABL ;color masking table
LDA #$00
ADC YTABL+1
STA COLTABL+1
CLC
LDA COLTABL
ADC #$08 ;Get starting loc for
STA POSTABL ;bit position table
LDA #$00
ADC COLTABL+1
STA POSTABL+1
CLC
LDA POSTABL
ADC #$07 ;Get starting loc for
STA XDIVTBL ;X/7 table
LDA #$00
ADC POSTABL+1
STA XDIVTBL+1
CLC
LDA XDIVTBL
ADC #$96 ;Get starting loc for
STA XMODTBL ;(X MOD 14)/2 table
LDA #$01
ADC XDIVTBL+1
STA XMODTBL+1
RTS
LST OFF
```

VI. A Tool or Three

Now that we have the groundwork laid out let's get to work. The HGR and HGR2 commands perform very similar functions in Applesoft, HGR displays and clears High-Res page one and sets the current plotting color to black ($00), HGR2 does the same thing but on High-Res page two, The only other difference between the two is that HGR sets mixed text and graphics mode, and HGR2 sets full-screen graphics mode. Another potentially useful function missing from Applesoft is one that would clear the current High-Res page to any desired color. Is it possible that we could kill all three birds with one stone?

Listing 1.3 shows that the answer is yes. By carefully coding the routine and providing three separate entry points, we can accomplish all three tasks with the same routine. Again for consistency, we'll choose to make both the HGR and HGR2 routines set full-screen graphics mode. Let's take a close look at the routines contained in Listing 3. The instructions at the HGR2 entry point cause page two of High-Res graphics to be displayed and the A-register to be loaded with a value of $40 before branching around the code for the HGR entry point. For HGR, a value of $20 is loaded into A and High-Res page one is displayed.

We have now reached the label HCLEAR with either a $20 or a $40 in the A register. Recall that High-Res page one starts at $2000 and page two starts at $4000. The value in A then is simply the high byte of the start address of the graphics page to be manipulated. This value is stored immediately in the location HGRPG. HGRPG is a very special page zero location that will always point to the High-Res page currently being read or written (but not necessarily displayed). It will be used extensively by other routines. Next we tweak all the switches necessary to set up full page, High-Res graphics, and then load A with the color to be used in filling the screen black.

Now we're at the third of our function entry points. If we jump directly to BKGND with the color (0-7) to be used in filling the screen in the A register, we can skip all the set-up work performed by HGR and HGR2 and take advantage of the same code they use to fill the screen with zeros (black0). At this point we transfer the contents of A into Y and do an indirect indexed load of the A-register using COLTABL. COLTABL is another page zero location, set up by the INIT routine to point to the start of the color mask table. This loads the appropriate color mask byte for the specified color from our lookup table. The color mask value becomes our current plotting color and is stored in two locations, COLOR and COLI where it can be found later. It's also stored in the location SHFTCHK where it can be found and used by the SHFTCOL routine.

Remember when we were discussing the on-off-on bit patterns earlier? We discovered that there are seven pixels per byte, right? This implies that we need to be careful in order to maintain a pattern of on-off-on through several bytes. If we have 1010101 for the first byte and for the second byte, the concatenated result is 10101011010101, clearly not what we want. What we need is a 1010101 followed by a 0101010 and so on. This one-bit shift is necessary to maintain the proper color masking pattern for all the bytes in a row and is precisely the function performed by the SHFTCOL routine.

Upon returning from SHFTCOL, the shifted color mask is loaded from SHFTCHK and stored in COL2. We now have everything we need and the rest of the routine is straightforward. A big loop is set up and all we need to do is copy COL1 into all the even bytes and COL2 into all the odd bytes of the High-Res screen indicated by HGRPG.

Listing 1.3 - HGR and HGR2 Subroutines

```
*
* The HGR and HGR2 subroutines function almost
*   identically to their Applesoft counterparts.
* No arguments need be passed to HGR and HGR2.
* To use BKGND, store the color (0-7) to clear the
*   screen to in A, then JSR BKGND.
*
 ORG $85B

SHFTCHK = $1C
TEMPPTR = $26
COLOR = $E4
HGRPG = $E6
COLTABL = $FE
DISPGR = $C050
NOMIX = $C052
DISPG1 = $C054
DISPG2 = $C055
```

11

```
      HIRES = $C057

COL1 DS 1
COL2 DS 1
TEMPCNT DS 1

HGR2 BIT DISPG2 ;Display hi-res pg 2
 LDA #$40 ;Hi byte of base adrs for pg2
 BNE HCLEAR
HGR LDA #$20 ;Hibyt of base adrs for pg1
 BIT DISPG1 ;Display hi-res pg1
HCLEAR BIT NOMIX ;Set all graphics mode
 STA HGRPG ;Store base adrs in HGRpg
 LDA HIRES ;Set HIRES mode
 LDA DISPGR ;Display graphics page
 LDA #$00 ;COLOR=Black0
BKGND TAY
 LDA (COLTABL),Y
 STA COLOR
 STA COL1
 STA SHFTCHK
 JSR SHFTCOL ;Shift color masking byte
 LDA SHFTCHK
 STA COL2
 LDA HGRPG ;Clear correct HGR page
 STA TEMPPTR+1
 LDA #0
 STA TEMPPTR
 LDA #$20 ;Hi byte of loop limit
 STA TEMPCNT
FILLSCR LDY #$FF
LOOP1A LDA COL1 ;Store col1 in even bytes
 STA (TEMPPTR),Y
 DEY
 LDA COL2 ;Store col2 in odd bytes
 STA (TEMPPTR),Y
 DEY
 CPY #$FF
 BNE LOOP1A ;Loop back for more
 INC TEMPPTR+1 ;Increment hi byte of ptr
 DEC TEMPCNT ;Dec. hi byte of loop count
 BNE FILLSCR
 RTS
SHFTCOL ASL
 CMP #$C0 ;Shift color masking
```

```
 BPL DONE ;byte routine for
 LDA SHFTCHK ;odd and even
 EOR #$7F ;screen bytes
 STA SHFTCHK
DONE RTS
 LST OFF
```

VII. A Demo Program

Let's write a little demo program and finish up. The first thing we need to do is decide where to put our lookup tables, so for lack of a better location let's assume that they will be loaded at $IBOO Gust below High-Res page one). For this reason, you will need to BLOAD YTABLE, A$1B00 as well as loading the INIT and HGR routines at their ORG addresses prior to BRUNning this demo. The first thing we need to do in the demo program is call INIT with the address of the YTABLE in A and X. This is taken care of by the first three lines of the program in Listing 1.4.

At this point, we can invoke any of the routines in our toolkit. Since we need to clear the screen and initialize High-Res graphics mode, the first thing we do is a]SR HGR. Next we'll set up a short loop and do a]SR BKGND for each of the eight HighRes colors. This will show how rapidly the High-Res screen can be cleared to any color you like. The implementation of the lookup tables makes our routine significantly faster than the standard Applesoft HGR routine. You may also want to change the JSR HGR to a JSR HGR2 to verify that the BKGND routine
will work on High-Res page 2 as well.

Listing 1.4 - Demo Program 1

```
*
* Title: Demo Program 1
* Function: Test INIT, HGR, HGR2 and BKGND routines
*
 ORG $6000

INIT EQU $803
HGR2 EQU $85E
HGR EQU $865
```

13

```
BKGND EQU $877

DEMO1 LDA #$1B ;Load A with YTABLE adr hi
 LDX #$00 ;Load X with YTABLE adr lo
 JSR INIT ;Set up lookup table ptrs
 JSR HGR ;Init hi-res graphics on page 1
 LDA #$00 ;Starting color is 0 (black0)
 STA COLORNO ;Save it for later use
LOOP LDA COLORNO ;Load color number for BKGND
 CMP #$08 ;See if we're done
 BEQ DONE ;If so, branch to DONE
 JSR BKGND ;Else do BKGND one more time
 INC COLORNO ;Do next color
 BNE LOOP ;Branch always to LOOP
DONE RTS

COLORNO DS 1
```

VIII. What to Expect Department

Where do we go from here? The difference between the routines in
Listings 1.2 and 1.3 and the routine in Listing 4 is that the first two are
tools and the last is an application that utilizes those tools. For the
demo program, we identified a problem to solve, namely, to
sequentially clear the graphics screen to each of the eight High-Res
colors. The tools we developed earlier helped us to solve our
problem.

During the course of this series, we'll be developing more tools that
can be used to solve graphics applications problems on the Apple II.
You can decide for yourself how to organize this library of useful
subroutines. If you type in all of them, the ORG addresses will all fit
nicely together and you'll have a good-sized library, that, with the
lookup tables, just fits under High-Res page 1. This leaves the largest
contiguous memory block in the Apple, from $6000-$9600, available
for applications programs.

Alternatively, you can use only those routines you need and assemble
them anywhere in memory, but be careful about declaring all the
addresses and variables. I needed to make each routine work.
Some, like INIT, are needed for any of the routines to work, and
nearly all will depend on the lookup tables. Take some time to absorb
all this, and we'll dive into it again in the next chapter!

CHAPTER 2

You will recall that previously we discussed some of the basics of Apple graphics and laid the groundwork for building our collection of machine language subroutines. We developed a lookup table, called the YTABLE, that will significantly speed up a lot of our graphics routines. We also came up with four routines (INIT, HGR, HGR2, and BKGND) to start off our toolkit. We'll look at three more routines: HCOLOR, HPLOT and HPOSN and write a short program to test these new routines.

State Elements

Your Apple II *is* a finite state machine, that is, a machine that can only be in one of a finite number of states at a given instant. You can think of the Apple as containing a very long string of binary digits (bits). Whenever any bit is changed, the state of the machine changes. Each bit is then a "state element" an atomic element of the machine, that, when changed, implies the state of the machine is changed as well.

What we are dealing with in this series is a subset of the Apple's memory space that looks like a simple graphics machine. State elements in this graphics machine include such things as the current color and the current position. When either of these change, the graphics machine is in a different state.

Two of the routines we'll talk about are responsible for modifying state elements in the graphics machine. HCOLOR, as you may have guessed, will allow us to change the current plotting color and HPOSN will let us change the current plotting position. The third routine, HPLOT, modifies two state elements. First, it calls HPOSN to set a new current position, then it modifies the pixel at that position. Each pixel in the memory of our graphics machine is also a state element.

HCOLOR, as you can see, is a very simple routine. It is passed a value from 0-7 in the A-register, transfers that value to the Y-register, then does an indirect indexed load, using the pointer to the color table. The color table (part of YTABLE) contains just eight bytes which are color masking bytes for each of the eight high-res colors.

15

This value is then stored in the location COLOR and will be used for all subsequent point and line drawing operations.

It should be noted here that in the interests of efficiency, very little checking is performed on the values passed to these graphics routines. If you pass HCOLOR a value of 147, expect to get something weird when you draw on the screen!

Let's take a look at HPOSN next. The purpose of HPOSN is to change the current position to the position of the point passed in the registers. This can be used to position one endpoint of a line or plot a single point. What do we need to do to calculate the byte address given a high-res screen coordinate? First we need to get the base address of the row. This is done using a table lookup as explained in the PART 1. The low byte of the base address is obtained directly from the table using the y-coordinate as an index. The high byte is obtained similarly, then OR'd with the current value of HGRPG. The resultant two-byte address is the address of the first byte of the row we want. This address is stored in TEMPPTR.

We can now use the XDIVTBL and XMODTBL values from the table in order to calculate the precise byte position and bit position within that byte. One complication arises since the two X tables are greater than 256 bytes long. Each of the X table pointers is incremented by one if the x-coordinate is greater than 256. Later on, we'll need to decrement these pointers if they are incremented here. The XDIVTBL pointer gets us the value of xl7 so that we can get a byte offset to calculate the precise address needed. Since there are 40 bytes of memory per high-res screen row, we'll get a value from 0-39. This byte offset value is then stored inn BYTENUM.

The XMODTBL pointer is also indexed by the x-coordinate to obtain the value of x mod 7 + 1. We now subtract one to get a value in the range 0-6 and use that as an index into the pixel position table. This gives us a mask for the position of the bit within the byte. This masking value is stored in POSBIT. Now, with the values of TEMPPTR, BYTENUM, and POSBIT, we know the precise location in memory of the high-res coordinate specified.

There is one more operation that HPOSN performs before returning. Remember our discussion last time about how the bit pattern needed to be shifted in order to maintain a constant on-off-on-off pattern from one byte to the next? HPOSN checks to see if BYTENUM is odd or even. If it is odd, the current color mask byte is shifted so that we get the right color. Whether it's shifted or not, the correct color mask value is left in SHFTCHK.

HPLOT now has it easy. The only trick is to plot the new point in the desired screen memory byte without affecting the other six pixels in that byte. HPLOT calls HPOSN, passing on the values in the registers. When HPOSN returns, TEMPPTR, BYTENUM, and POSBIT are all set up. The current color mask is loaded from SHFTCHK and the Y register is loaded with the value of BYTENUM to be used as an offset. The color mask byte is exclusive-OR'd with the contents of the correct high-res screen memory byte, ANDed with the pixel position mask (POSBIT), exclusive-OR'd with the high-res screen memory byte again, and the result is stored in screen memory.

In order to plot the point in the correct color, the color flag of the screen memory byte must be set to the same value as the color flag of the current color. This may affect the other six pixels in the byte, causing the well-known "bleeding" problem. To illustrate this, run the following short Applesoft program:

```
10 HGR: HCOLOR=5
20 HPLOT 0,50 TO 279,50
30 HCOLOR=1
40 HPLOT 100,50
```

The Demo Program

Listing 2.2 contains a demo program that lets you test out the new routines. You will have to BLOAD YTABLE, A$1B00 and then BLOAD the INIT and HGR routines we developed last time. Now you can BLOAD the routines in Listing 1 and you're all set to BRUN the program in Listing 2.

It should draw two diagonal lines, one orange and one blue. They will appear dotted since certain colors cannot be seen in even columns and others cannot be seen in odd columns. Try modifying the program to draw white lines so that the lines look smoother.

17

Listing 2.1 - Toolkit Routines

```
 ORG $8BC
SHFTCHK EQU $1C
TEMPPTR EQU $26
POSBIT EQU $30
POSTABL EQU $4A
XDIVTBL EQU $4C
XMODTBL EQU $D0
OLDXLO EQU $E0
OLDXHI EQU $E1
OLDY EQU $E2
COLOR EQU $E4
BYTENUM EQU $E5
HGRPG EQU $E6
YTABL EQU $EC
YTABH EQU $EE
COLTABL EQU $FE
PIXPOS DS 1
SHFTCOL EQU $8B0
*
*   THE HCOLOR ROUTINE WILL CHANGE THE
*   CURRENT PLOTTING COLOR TO THE COLOR (0-7)
*   THAT IS PASSED IN THE A REGISTER
*
HCOLOR TAY
 LDA (COLTABL),Y ;LOAD APPROPRIATE COLOR MASK BYTE
 STA COLOR ;SAVE IT FOR FUTURE USE
 RTS
*
*   CALL HPLOT WITH A POINT TO BE PLOTTED.
*   THE HIGH BYTE OF THE X-COORDINATE SHOULD
*   BE PASSED IN THE A REGISTER, X-LO IN THE
*   X REGISTER, AND THE Y-COORDINATE IN THE
*   Y REGISTER.
*
HPLOT JSR HPOSN ;FIND PIXEL ADRS
 LDA SHFTCHK ;AND CORRECT COLOR MASK
 LDY BYTENUM
 EOR (TEMPPTR),Y
 AND POSBIT ;TURN ON CORRECT POINT
 EOR (TEMPPTR),Y
 STA (TEMPPTR),Y ;STORE BYTE BACK ON SCREEN
 RTS
```

```
*
*  CALL HPOSN WITH A POINT TO POSITIONED BUT
*  NOT PLOTTED.  THIS POINT SHOULD BE PASSED
*  IN THE SAME MANNER AS HPLOT (DESCRIBED ABOVE).
*
HPOSN STA OLDXHI ;SAVE X-HI
 STX OLDXLO ;SAVE X-LO
 STY OLDY ;SAVE Y
 LDA (YTABL),Y
 STA TEMPPTR ;FIND Y BASE ADRS
 LDA (YTABH),Y
 ORA HGRPG ;GET CORRECT HGRPG
 STA TEMPPTR+1 ;STORE ADRS IN TEMPPTR
 LDY OLDXHI
 BEQ LT256B
 INC XDIVTBL+1 ;INCREMENT XTABLE PTRS BY
 PAG
 INC XMODTBL+1 ;ONE PAGE IF X>255
LT256B LDY OLDXLO
 LDA (XDIVTBL),Y
 STA BYTENUM ;FIND BYTE POSITION IN ROW
 LDY OLDXLO
 LDA (XMODTBL),Y
 TAY
 DEY
 LDA (POSTABL),Y
 STA POSBIT ;FIND PIXEL POSITION IN BYTE
 STY PIXPOS
 LDA OLDXHI
 BEQ LT256D
 DEC XDIVTBL+1 ;RESTORE XTABLE PTRS IF
 DEC XMODTBL+1 ;X WAS > 255
LT256D LDA BYTENUM
 CLC
 LSR
 LDA COLOR ;SHIFT COLOR MASKING
 STA SHFTCHK ;BYTE IF NECESSARY
 BCS SHFTCOL
 RTS
```

Listing 2.2 - Toolkit Demo 2

```
* TITLE: DEMO PROGRAM 2
* FUNCTION: TEST HCOLOR, HPLOT AND HPOSN ROUTINES
* AUTHOR:   RANDI J. ROST
* DATE:     16-OCT-83

 ORG $6000
INIT EQU $803
HGR2 EQU $85E
HGR EQU $865
BKGND EQU $877
HCOLOR EQU $8BD
HPLOT EQU $8C3
HPOSN EQU $8D3
DEMO2 LDA #$1B ;LOAD A WITH YTABLE ADR HI
 LDX #$00 ;LOAD X WITH YTABLE ADR LO
 JSR INIT ;SET UP LOOKUP TABLE PTRS
 JSR HGR ;INIT HI-RES GRAPHICS ON PAGE 1
 LDA #05 ;CHANGE PLOTTING COLOR TO ORANGE
 JSR HCOLOR
 LDA #191 ;INIT (X,Y) TO (191,191)
 STA TEMPX
 STA TEMPY
LOOP1 LDA #0
 LDX TEMPX
 LDY TEMPY ;DRAW LINE FROM (191,191) TO (0,0)
 JSR HPLOT
 DEC TEMPX
 DEC TEMPY
 BNE LOOP1
 LDA #06 ;CHANGE PLOTTING COLOR TO BLUE
 JSR HCOLOR
 LDA #191
 STA TEMPX
LOOP2 LDA #0
 LDX TEMPX
 LDY TEMPY
 JSR HPLOT ;DRAW LINE FROM (191,0) TO (0,191)
 INC TEMPY
 DEC TEMPX
 BNE LOOP2
 RTS
TEMPX DS 1
TEMPY DS 1
A
```

20

Next Time

In Chapter 3, we'll look at line-drawing algorithms and improve slightly on the one that Applesoft uses. After that, we'll be jumping into animation-quality block-shape routines. I will begin to give less detailed descriptions of how the machine language routines work since they do have some comments and we'll need to spend more time explaining the philosophy behind the implementation.

CHAPTER 3

In the first two chapters we developed some simple routines to clear the screen, plot a point and so on, and laid the groundwork for more difficult routines to come. This time we'll look at line-drawing algorithms and present a disassembled, commented version of the line-drawing routine used within Applesoft.

Line-Drawing

One of the earliest graphics problems involved computing which pixels to turn on to give the most reasonable approximation of a line between two points. Three of the criteria for a good line-drawing algorithm are:

1. Lines should appear straight
2. Lines should terminate accurately
3. Lines should be drawn rapidly

There are some other considerations as well, but these three are the most pertinent to the two algorithms we'll look at here.

The Simple DDA

Your first attempt at developing a line-drawing algorithm might lead you to come up with one similar to the simple DDA, or digital differential analyzer. The algorithm stems from the fact that differential equations of the lines themselves are used to generate the line. For straight lines we have a very simple equation:

$$\frac{DY}{DX} \quad = \quad \text{Delta y / delta x}$$

$$= \quad (y2-y1)/(x2-x1)$$

$$= \quad \text{Slope of line}$$

23

The algorithm then works on the principal that we increment the current plotting position each iteration by a value proportional to the slope of the line. In the case of the simple DDA, the number of points to be plotted is assumed to be the larger of abs(dx) +1 and abs(dy) + 1 where (x1,y1) and (x2,y2) are the endpoints of the line to be drawn and dx=x2-x1 and dy=y2-y1.

Values for Xinc and Yinc are then computed such that Yinc/Xinc = slope, and at least one of Xinc and Yinc is unit magnitude (1 or -1). Since we are also dealing with a grid of points addressed by integers, we'll have to round off floating point numbers to integers before plotting points.

The simple DDA algorithm first calculates the number of points to be plotted as well as values for Xinc and Yinc and accomplishes rounding by adding a value of 0.5 to the starting x and y positions. The first point is obtained by taking the integer value of the starting x and y positions. After the first point is plotted, Xinc and Yinc are added to the current position, the integer value is taken, the point is plotted and the process repeats until the previously calculated number of points has been plotted. Listing 1 shows an implementation of the simple DDA algorithm in Applesoft BASIC.

Listing 3.1 - Simple DDA Algorithm

```
100  TEXT : HOME : VTAB 10
110  PRINT "INPUT X1,Y1";: INPUT X1,Y1
120  PRINT "INPUT X2,Y2";: INPUT X2,Y2
130 DX = X2 - X1:DY = Y2 - Y1
140 AX =  ABS (DX):AY =  ABS (DY)
150 COUNT = AX
160  IF AY <  = AX THEN 180
170 COUNT = AY
180 EX = DX / COUNT:EY = DY / COUNT
190  HGR : HCOLOR= 3
200  FOR I = 0 TO COUNT
210  HPLOT  INT (X1 + 0.5), INT (Y1 + 0.5)
220 X1 = X1 + EX
230 Y1 = Y1 + EY
240  NEXT I
```

Bresenham's Algorithm

As everyone who's tinkered at the level of bits and bytes knows, integer arithmetic is much faster than floating point arithmetic on machines with no floating point hardware. In addition, adds and subtracts are significantly faster than multiplies and divides on machines with no multiply or divide instructions. Many microcomputers, including the Apple II, are based on microprocessors that contain neither multiply and divide instructions nor floating point capability. J.E. Bresenham came up with an algorithm that runs significantly faster than the simple DDA algorithm on such machines since it requires only additions, subtractions, and multiplication by two (which can be performed with a rotate instruction).

Bresenham's algorithm is like the simple DDA in that each iteration changes one of the coordinates by 1 or -1. For each iteration, the other coordinate mayor may not change, depending on the error term maintained by the algorithm. For cases where dx < dy, this error term is initialized to abs(dx)*2 -dy, and for dx >=dy it is initialized to abs(dy)*2 dx. This forces the error term to be negative. Each time a point is plotted a value of dx*2 (for the first case) or dy*2 (for the second case) is added to the error term. When the error term becomes positive, it is time to increment the other coordinate as well. Listing 3.2 is an Applesoft implementation of Bresenham's algorithm.

Listing 3.2 - Bresenham's Algorithm in Applesoft

```
100  TEXT : HOME : VTAB 10
110  PRINT "INPUT X1,Y1";: INPUT X1,Y1
120  PRINT "INPUT X2,Y2";: INPUT X2,Y2
130  HGR : HCOLOR= 3
140 DX = X2 - X1:XINC = 1
150  IF DX >  = 0 THEN 170
160 DX =   - DX:XINC =   - 1
170 DY = Y2 - Y1:YINC = 1
180  IF DY >  = 0 THEN 200
190 DY =   - DY:YINC =   - 1
200  IF DX < DY THEN 290
205  REM  ** CASE WHERE DX >= DY **
210 ERR = DY * 2 - DX
220  HPLOT X1,Y1
```

```
230 X1 = X1 + XINC: IF X1 = X2 THEN 370
240 ERR = ERR + DY * 2
250  IF ERR <  = 0 THEN 220
260 Y1 = Y1 + YINC
270 ERR = ERR - DX * 2
280  GOTO 220
285  REM  ** CASE WHERE DX < DY **
290 ERR = DX * 2 - DY
300  HPLOT X1,Y1
310 Y1 = Y1 + YINC: IF Y1 = Y2 THEN 370
320 ERR = ERR + DX * 2
330  IF ERR <  = 0 THEN 300
340 X1 = X1 + XINC
350 ERR = ERR - DY * 2
360  GOTO 300
370  HPLOT X2,Y2
380  END
```

Applesoft's Line-Drawing Routine

Listing 3.3 contains a disassembled version of Applesoft's line-drawing routine, with a few minor changes. I have utilized a YTABLE look-up to speed up the algorithm slightly. I did try writing my own line-drawing routine, but I found that the routine that Applesoft uses to draw lines takes such good advantage of the Apple's peculiar architecture that it was tough to improve upon it. If you're curious, the original routine can be found in memory starting at location $F53A.

Your mission is to count the number of cute tricks that were used to make the routine more efficient. I will point out a few to give you the flavor of what can be done. One of the most useful speed-up tricks is the use of in-line code. This line-drawing routine could be written using a call to HPLOT, but that would involve the execution of at least two more instructions-a JSR to call the subroutine and an RTS to return. Instead, the code for HPLOT can be duplicated within the HUNE routine wherever needed since it is so short, thus saving a few precious cycles each time a point is plotted.

Another trick that is used successfully in this routine is the manner by which screen address calculation is avoided unless absolutely necessary. Recall that information about seven pixels is stored in a single byte of the Apple's screen memory. If the next point to be plotted is one dot left or right of the point last plotted, there's a good chance that the pixel is contained in the same byte as the last one was and the position within the byte is all that needs to be changed.

Look for these and other speed-up techniques used in the line-drawing routine used by Applesoft. It is basically the Bresenham algorithm with some Apple-specific quirks. Follow along with the Applesoft listing of the algorithm in Listing 3.2, and note the sections of the assembly language listing that correspond to the Applesoft implementation.

Why do we need a line-drawing routine in our toolkit anyway? Why can't we just use the one built into the Apple? Well, for one thing, there are still a few people around (like me!) who have the antique Apple II's with Integer Basic in ROM instead of Applesoft. For another, we want our toolkit to contain all the tools we will be needing, and we want them to be consistent with all the other tools. And finally, we want to learn more about line-drawing algorithms so that we can implement them on other machines as well.

Listing 3.3 — Graphics Toolkit Subroutines

```
*********************************************************
*            HI-RES GRAPHICS SUBROUTINES             *
*                        BY                          *
*                  RANDI J. ROST                     *
*                    6/30/82                         *
*      COPYRIGHT (C) 1983  BY CALL-A.P.P.L.E         *
*   NOT TO BE USED IN COMMERCIAL PROGRAMS WITHOUT    *
*    THE CONSENT OF THE AUTHOR AND A.P.P.L.E.        *
*********************************************************
 ORG $911
SHFTCHK EQU $1C
TEMPPTR EQU $26
POSBIT EQU $30
LOOPLIM EQU $1D
OLDXLO EQU $E0
OLDXHI EQU $E1
OLDY EQU $E2
BYTENUM EQU $E5
HGRPG EQU $E6
COLCTR EQU $EA
```

```
YTABL EQU $EC
YTABH EQU $EE
DTEMPX DS 1
DTEMPY DS 1
OLDY2 DS 1
ABSDXLO DS 1
ABSDXHI DS 1
ABSDY DS 1
DXHI DS 1
ERRLO DS 1
ERRHI DS 1
*
*  HLINE WILL DRAW A LINE IN THE CURRENT PLOTTING
*  COLOR FROM THE POINT LAST HPOSN'ED OR HPLOTTED
*  TO THE POINT PASSED IN THE REGISTERS AS FOLLOWS-
*  XHI IN A, XLO IN X, AND Y IN Y.
*
HLINE STA DTEMPX ;TWIDDLE REGISTERS TO ALLOW
 LDA OLDY ;OPTIMAL SPEED IN ALGORITHM
 STA OLDY2 ;SAVE OLDY AS A REFERENCE PT
 TXA
 LDX DTEMPX
 PHA   ;SAVE XLO ON STACK
 SEC
 SBC OLDXLO ;NEWXLO - OLDXLO
 PHA   ;SAVE DXLO ON STACK
 TXA
 SBC OLDXHI ;NEWXHI - OLDXHI
 STA DXHI
 BCS DXNOTNEG
 PLA   ;GET ABS(DX) IF
 EOR #$FF ;DX < 0
 ADC #$01
 PHA
 LDA #$00
 SBC DXHI
DXNOTNEG STA ABSDXHI
 STA ERRHI ;SAVE ABS(DX) HI BYTE
 PLA
 STA ABSDXLO
 STA ERRLO ;SAVE ABS(DX) LO BYTE
 PLA
 STA OLDXLO
 STX OLDXHI
 TYA
```

```
         CLC
         SBC OLDY ;NEWY - OLDY
         BCC DYNOTNEG
         EOR #$FF ;GET ABS(DY) IF DY < 0
         ADC #$FE
DYNOTNEG STA ABSDY
         STY OLDY
         ROR DXHI
         SEC
         SBC ABSDXLO
         TAX
         LDA #$FF
         SBC ABSDXHI ;CALCULATE LOOPLIMIT
         STA LOOPLIM
         LDY BYTENUM
         BCS SKIPINCX
INCXLOOP ASL
         JSR DECRX ;GO INCREMENT (OR DEC) X POS.
         SEC
SKIPINCX LDA ERRLO
         ADC ABSDY
         STA ERRLO
         LDA ERRHI
         SBC #$00
PLOTMORE STA ERRHI
         LDA (TEMPPTR),Y ;LOAD CURRENT CONTENTS
         EOR SHFTCHK ;SCREEN BYTE, EOR IT WITH
         AND POSBIT ;COLOR BYTE, AND IT WITH
         EOR (TEMPPTR),Y ;POSBIT, EOR WITH SCREEN
         STA (TEMPPTR),Y ;AGAIN AND PUT IT BACK.
         INX
         BNE NOTDONE
         INC LOOPLIM
         BEQ HLDONE ;WE'RE DONE WHEN LOOPLIM=0
NOTDONE  LDA DXHI
         BCS INCXLOOP
         JSR INCRY ;NOW GO INC (OR DEC) Y
         CLC
         LDA ERRLO
         ADC ABSDXLO
         STA ERRLO
         LDA ERRHI
         ADC ABSDXHI
         BVC PLOTMORE ;GO BACK FOR MORE PTS
HLDONE   RTS
```

29

```
DECRX BPL INCRX ;IF INC VALUE > 0 GO INCREMENT
 LDA POSBIT ;IF NOT, DECREMENT PIXEL
 LSR   ;POSITION BYTE
 BCS DECBYTNO ;IF SHIFT TOO FAR, DEC BYTENUM
 EOR #$C0 ;TURN BIT 7 ON, BIT 6 OFF
DECDONE1 STA POSBIT ;STORE RESULT BACK IN POSBIT
 RTS
DECBYTNO DEY   ;DECREMENT BYTE # IN ROW
 BPL NOWRAP
 LDY #$27 ;WRAP AROUND IF X<0
NOWRAP LDA #$C0 ;AND BITS 6 & 7 ARE ON
STOREPOS STA POSBIT ;IN POSITION BYTE
 STY BYTENUM ;AND IN BYTE # COUNTER
 LDA SHFTCHK
 ASL   ;SHIFT COLOR MASKING BYTE
 CMP #$C0
 BPL DECDONE2
 LDA SHFTCHK
 EOR #$7F ;DO THE COLOR SHIFT IF NEC.
 STA SHFTCHK
DECDONE2 RTS
INCRX LDA POSBIT
 ASL   ;SHIFT POSBIT LEFT TO
 EOR #$80 ;INCREMENT X (LEAVE BIT 7 ON)
 BMI DECDONE1
 LDA #$81 ;SHIFTED OUT OF CURRENT BYTE
 INY   ;SO INCREMENT BYTE #
 CPY #$28 ;BUT NOT PASSED 40 (X=280)
 BCC STOREPOS
 LDY #$00 ;WRAPAROUND IF X>279
 BCS STOREPOS
 CLC
 LDA ABSDXHI
 AND #$04
 BEQ SKIPPLOT
 LDA #$7F ;SEE IF NEW POINT COLLIDES
 AND POSBIT ;WITH ANOTHER ON THE SCREEN
 AND (TEMPPTR),Y
 BNE PLOTPT
 INC COLCTR
 LDA #$7F
 AND POSBIT
 BPL PLOTPT
 CLC
 LDA ABSDXHI
```

```
 AND #$04
 BEQ SKIPPLOT
 LDA (TEMPPTR),Y
 EOR SHFTCHK
 AND POSBIT
 BNE PLOTPT
 INC COLCTR
PLOTPT EOR (TEMPPTR),Y
 STA (TEMPPTR),Y ;PLOT THE POINT
SKIPPLOT LDA ABSDXHI
 ADC DXHI
 AND #$03
 CMP #$02
 ROR
 BCS DECRX ;GO BACK FOR MORE
INCRY BMI DECRY ;DECREMENT Y IF INDEX < 0
 STY DTEMPY ;SAVE BYTE POSITION
 DEC OLDY2 ;DEC CURRENT Y VALUE
 LDY OLDY2 ;LOAD IT INTO INDEX REG
 CPY #$FF ;SEE IF WE'RE OFF TOP OF SCRN
 BNE LT192 ;IF NOT, SKIP
 LDY #191 ;ELSE WRAPAROUND TO BOTTOM
 STY OLDY2 ;SAVE AS CURRENT Y
LT192 LDA (YTABL),Y ;GET Y BASE ADDRESS FROM TABLE
 STA TEMPPTR
 LDA (YTABH),Y
 ORA HGRPG ;GET CORRECT HGRPG
 STA TEMPPTR+1
 LDY DTEMPY ;RESTORE BYTENUM
 RTS
DECRY STY DTEMPY ;SAVE BYTENUM FOR LATER
 INC OLDY2 ;INCREMENT Y POSITION
 LDY OLDY2 ;LOAD IT FOR INDEXING YTABLE
 CPY #192 ;ARE WE OFF BOTTOM EDGE?
 BNE GT0
 LDY #0 ;IF SO, WRAPAROUND
 STY OLDY2 ;SAVE AS CURRENT Y LOC.
GT0 LDA (YTABL),Y ;LOAD Y BASE ADDRESS FROM TABLE
 STA TEMPPTR
 LDA (YTABH),Y
 ORA HGRPG ;GET CORRECT HGRPG
 STA TEMPPTR+1
 LDY DTEMPY ;RESTORE BYTENUM
 RTS
```

31

The Demo Program

Another short demo program is included as Listing 3.4. Before running the demo program, you must load the Y TABLE and the other toolkit routines we have developed.

Again, keep in mind that the demo program is essentially an "applications" program. Its only desire is to use the graphics subroutines we have developed so far. An application should be able to use the toolkit routines given only the starting addresses of the routines and the conventions for passing arguments.

Applications programs don't need to know any thing about the internal operation of the toolkit routines. Next time we'll take a look at setting up a graphics "window" and do a few special effects. After that we'll begin talking about shape tables and routines needed to do arcade-quality animation on the Apple.

Listing 3.4 - Demo Program 3

```
*
* TITLE: DEMO PROGRAM 3
* FUNCTION: TEST HCOLOR, HPOSN AND HLINE ROUTINES
* AUTHOR:   RANDI J. ROST
* DATE:     10-JUN-84
*
*
 ORG $6000
INIT EQU $803
HGR EQU $865
HCOLOR EQU $8BD
HPOSN EQU $8D3
HLINE EQU $91A
DEMO3 LDA #$1B ;LOAD A WITH YTABLE ADR HI
 LDX #$00 ;LOAD X WITH YTABLE ADR LO
 JSR INIT ;SET UP LOOKUP TABLE PTRS
 JSR HGR ;INIT HI-RES GRAPHICS ON PAGE 1
 LDA #191 ;INIT Y TO 191
 STA TEMPY
LOOP LDA TEMPY ;LOAD CURRENT Y VALUE
  AND #7 ;MASK OFF ALL BUT BOTTOM 3 BITS
 JSR HCOLOR ;USE THIS AS PLOT COLOR
 LDA #0 ;XHI = 0
 LDX #0 ;XLO = 0
 LDY TEMPY ;LOAD CURRENT Y VALUE
 JSR HPOSN ;POSITION ENDPOINT 1
 LDA #1 ;XHI = 1
 LDX #23 ;XLO = 23 (XVALUE = 279)
 LDY TEMPY ;LOAD CURRENT Y VALUE
 JSR HLINE ;DRAW THE HORIZONTAL LINE
 DEC TEMPY ;DECREMENT CURRENT Y VALUE
 BNE LOOP ;DRAW MORE IF Y <> 0
 RTS  ;ALL DONE!
TEMPY DS 1
T
```

CHAPTER 4

In the past three chapters, we developed routines to perform the most common graphics functions. This time, we'll talk about establishing a "graphics window" and present a routine that will perform some interesting operations on the contents of that window.

Graphics Windows

The term "window" has about as many meanings with respect to computer graphics as there are graphics programmers. The definition we will use is as follows: a window is a subset (usually rectangular) of the entire graphics screen, outside of which graphics commands have no effect. In other words, a rectangular subset of the graphics screen can be established as a graphics window, and the area outside the window will become immune to all graphics operations. Only the area inside the window can be affected by commands that draw lines or shapes.

This brings us to the subject of clipping. Clipping a line or shape involves discarding any part of the line or shape that is outside a specified boundary. For instance, it is useful to clip lines that would otherwise extend beyond the Apple's screen boundary of (0,0) to (279,191). Oftentimes the line-drawing algorithm causes unclipped lines that extend beyond the screen boundaries to "wraparound" to the other side of the screen.

As an example, let's consider a graphics device with a resolution of 256 x 256. The current location can be stored in two bytes, one byte for the current x position and the other for the y position. Now let's imagine drawing a line from 150,150 to 300,200. The algorithm that will draw lines will probably just plot points and increment the x and y values whenever necessary. But what happens when the x value is 255? Incrementing 255 gives 0 and the line will "wrap-around" to the left edge of the screen.

Applesoft clips lines by checking the endpoints that you provide. If either endpoint has an x-value less than 0 or greater than 279 or a y-value less than 0 or greater that 191, you are given an error message and no line is drawn. If you bypass Applesoft, you can succeed in giving the line-drawing routine values that will cause wraparound to occur. A more forgiving way to handle this problem would be to clip the lines.

Defining a window gives us greater flexibility. Clipping will be performed against the current window boundaries instead of against the screen boundaries. A couple of simple routines will allow us to change the boundaries of the window to anything we want.

Apple Eccentricities

We've already talked about how the Apple's graphics memory is organized, and its peculiarities will force us to make a concession here. Since each byte of graphics memory contains a color flag and on/off information for seven pixels, we'll save ourselves lots of computation and headaches by restricting the left and right window edges to fall on byte boundaries.

The subroutines in Listing 4.1 allow you to establish the current window by specifying the upper left corner and the lower right corner. The CHGUPLFT and CHGLOWRT routines will make sure the left and right edges of the window are on byte boundaries, even if the points you specified aren't.

You'll also want to add the following lines of code to the initialization routine so that the graphics window is set to the default full screen size when the INIT routine is called:

```
LDA -$00
TAX
TAY
JSR CHGUPLFT        ;INIT SCREEN WINDOW
LDA -$01            ;TO DEFAULT 280 X 192
LDX -$17
LDY -$BF
JSR CHGLOWRT
```

36

Listing 4.1 - Current Window

```
*   CHGUPLFT AND CHGLOWRT ARE USED TO CHANGE
*   THE GRAPHICS WINDOW BOUNDARIES.  SHAPES CAN
*   BE DRAWN ONLY WITHIN THE GRAPHICS WINDOW, AND
*   CMPLMNT ONLY AFFECTS VALUES INSIDE THE WINDOW.
*   CALL EITHER ROUTINE WITH THE COORDINATE OF THE NEW
*   GRAPHICS WINDOW CORNER (EITHER UPPER LEFT OR LOWER
*   RIGHT) WITH XHI IN A, XLO IN X, AND Y IN Y.


 ORG $A68
XDIVTBL EQU $4C
TEMPPTR2 EQU $D2
LFTXBYTE DS 1
RTXBYTE DS 1
WNDWTOP DS 1
WNDWBOT DS 1
WNDWRLO DS 1
WNDWRHI DS 1
WNDWLLO DS 1
WNDWLHI DS 1
CHGUPLFT STA WNDWLHI ;STORE WINDOW LEFT HIGH
 STX WNDWLLO ;STORE WINDOW LEFT LOW
 STY WNDWTOP ;STORE WINDOW TOP
 JSR GETXBYTE ;COMPUTE BYTE # OF LEFT EDGE
 STA LFTXBYTE ;STORE RESULT AS LEFT EDGE
 RTS  ;DONE!
CHGLOWRT STA WNDWRHI ;STORE WINDOW RIGHT HIGH
 STX WNDWRLO ;STORE WINDOW RIGHT LOW
 STY WNDWBOT ;STORE WINDOW BOTTOM
 JSR GETXBYTE ;COMPUTE RIGHT EDGE BYTE #
 STA RTXBYTE ;STORE RESULT
 RTS  ;DONE!
GETXBYTE LDY XDIVTBL
 STY TEMPPTR2
 LDY XDIVTBL+1 ;STORE POINTER TO XDIVTBL
 STY TEMPPTR2+1 ;IN TEMPPTR SO WE CAN COMPUTE
 TAY  ;THE VALUE OF X/7
 BEQ LT256XX
 INC TEMPPTR2+1
LT256XX TXA  ;USE VALUE OF X AS INDEX TO TABLE
 TAY
 LDA (TEMPPTR2),Y ;LOAD VALUE OF X/7 FROM TABLE
 RTS  ;DONE
S
```

37

Special Effects

The routine in Listing 4.2 is of questionable value, but add it to your library of routines anyway and someday you may find a use for it. The routine is based on the peculiarities of the Apple's graphics architecture we just mentioned. There are three ways we can modify a byte of graphics memory:

1. Invert the color flag
2. Invert the seven pixel values in the byte
3. Invert the color flag and the seven pixel values in the byte

The routine will perform one of the three "complements" on the current graphics window depending on the value passed in the A-register. The beauty is that a second complement of the same type will restore the screen to its original state. You may find this useful for explosions or "glitter" effects in title pages.

The CMPLMNT routine utilizes the sometimes useful, but always debatable technique of self-modifying cost. Since the three types of complements differ in only two EOR instructions, we can save a little space using this technique. The first part of the CMPLMNT routine stores the proper EOR instructions in the main loop of the routine depending on the value passed in the A-register. Self-modifying can be a dangerous thing (hard to find bugs!) but it can also save you a headache or some space once in a while.

Listing 4.2 - Questionable Routine

```
*   CMPLMNT WILL COMPLEMENT ALL THE COLORS
*   IN THE CURRENT GRAPHICS WINDOW. CALLING CMPLMNT
*   AGAIN WILL REVERT EVERYTHING BACK TO
*   ITS ORIGINAL VALUE.  PASS A 0, 1, OR 2 IN THE A
*   REGISTER DEPENDING ON WHICH TYPE OF COMPLEMENT IS
*   DESIRED.
*
 ORG $AA2
YTABL EQU $EC
YTABH EQU $EE
TEMPPTR EQU $26
HGRPG EQU $E6
LFTXBYTE EQU $A68
```

```
RTXBYTE EQU $A69
WNDWTOP EQU $A6A
WNDWBOT EQU $A6B
ROW DS 1
CMPLMNT TAX
 BEQ CMPLMNT0 ;BRANCH IF TYPE 0 COMPLEMENT
 LDA #$EA ;NOP-OUT SECOND EOR FOR TYPE
 STA CHGLOC+2 ;1 AND 2 COMPLEMENTS
 STA CHGLOC+3
 DEX
 BEQ CMPLMNT1 ;IF TYPE 1 COMPLEMENT, BRANCH
 LDA #$80 ;CHANGE FIRST EOR TO 'EOR #$80'
 BNE CMPCONT1 ;FOR TYPE 2 COMPLEMENT
CMPLMNT1 LDA #$FF ;CHANGE FIRST EOR TO 'EOR #$FF'
CMPCONT1 STA CHGLOC+1
 JMP CLOOP1 ;SKIP TYPE 0 COMPLEMENT STUFF
CMPLMNT0 LDA #$FF ;CHANGE FIRST EOR TO 'EOR #$FF'
 STA CHGLOC+1
 LDA #$49 ;LOAD OPCODE FOR EOR
 STA CHGLOC+2
 LDA #$80 ;CHANGE SECOND EOR TO 'EOR #$80'
 STA CHGLOC+3
CLOOP1 LDY WNDWTOP ;STARTING VALUE FOR OUTER LOOP
 STY ROW
CLOOP2 LDX RTXBYTE ;LIMIT OF INNER LOOP (40)
 LDA (YTABL),Y ;SCREEN, EOR'ING EACH
 STA TEMPPTR ;BYTE APPROPRIATELY.
 LDA (YTABH),Y
 ORA HGRPG
 STA TEMPPTR+1
 LDY LFTXBYTE
CLOOP3 LDA (TEMPPTR),Y ;SECOND TIME CHANGES
CHGLOC EOR #$FF ;EVERYTHING BACK TO
 EOR #$80 ;ITS ORIGINAL STATE
 STA (TEMPPTR),Y
 INY
 CPY RTXBYTE ;SEE IF INNER LOOP LIMIT REACHED
 BLT CLOOP3 ;IF NOT, BRANCH BACK FOR MORE
 BEQ CLOOP3
 INC ROW ;INCREMENT CURRENT ROW
 LDY ROW
 CPY WNDWBOT ;SEE IF WE'RE DONE
 BNE CLOOP2
 RTS  ;DONE
 ;
```

Demos Away!

Listing 4.3 is an example program that illustrates the use of CHGUPLFT, CHGLOWRT and CMPLMNT. After you have typed in the listing and assembled it successfully, do the following:

1. From Applesoft, type HGR to display and clear hi-res page 1.
2. BLOAD some hi-res picture you have stored on disk or run a program that generates a picture on page 1.
3. BLOAD all the toolkit routines, including those in Listings 1 and 2.
4. BRUN the demo program

Listing 4.3 — Demo Program 4

```
*
* TITLE: DEMO PROGRAM 4
* FUNCTION: TEST CHGUPLFT, CHGLOWRT, AND CMPLMNT ROUTINES
* AUTHOR:   RANDI J. ROST
* DATE:     28-JUL-84
*
*
 ORG $6000
INIT EQU $803
CHGUPLFT EQU $A70
CHGLOWRT EQU $A80
CMPLMNT EQU $AA3
DEMO4 LDA #$1B ;LOAD A WITH YTABLE ADR HI
 LDX #$00 ;LOAD X WITH YTABLE ADR LO
 JSR INIT ;SET UP LOOKUP TABLE PTRS
 LDA #00
 LDX #30
 LDY #30
 JSR CHGUPLFT ;CHANGE UPPER LEFT TO (30,30)
 LDA #0
 LDX #250
 LDY #162
 JSR CHGLOWRT ;CHANGE LOWER RIGHT TO (250,162)
 LDA #0
 JSR CMPLMNT ;DO A TYPE 0 COMPLEMENT
 LDX #255
 JSR DELAY ;PAUSE
 LDA #0
 JSR CMPLMNT ;RESTORE SCREEN
```

```
        LDA #1
        JSR CMPLMNT ;DO A TYPE 1 COMPLEMENT
        LDX #255
        JSR DELAY ;PAUSE
        LDA #1
        JSR CMPLMNT ;RESTORE SCREEN
        LDA #2
        JSR CMPLMNT ;DO A TYPE 2 COMPLEMENT
        LDX #255
        JSR DELAY ;PAUSE
        LDA #2
        JSR CMPLMNT ;RESTORE SCREEN
        RTS  ;DONE!
DELAY   LDY #255
DELAY2  DEY
        BNE DELAY2
        DEX
        BNE DELAY
        RTS
```

Till Next Time

When we develop our shape-drawing routines we'll be sure and include clipping against the window boundaries. None of the routines presented in other parts had provisions for doing such a thing. You may want to go back and alter the HPLOT, HLINE, and BKGND routines to include the window concept by clipping against the window boundary.

If you are keeping the routines as separate files on your development disk, be sure to keep your $ORG addresses straight so that the routines don't end up on top of each other.

$EQU's in demo programs will also have to be changed if start addresses of the toolkit routines change. There may also be other routines you want to add to this collection. One useful routine to add is the random number generator presented by David Sparks in the May 1982 issue of Call-A.P.P.L.E.. The INIT routine could be modified to make a call to RNDINIT to initialize the random number generator. a routine that quickly draws filled or hollow rectangles should also be possible at this point.

We now have routines that duplicate the graphics functionality of Applesoft and have a few freebies thrown in besides. In the next part, we'll talk about shapes for arcade-quality animation and develop an Applesoft program to generate shape tables.

CHAPTER 5

Getting Ready for Screen Animation

So far we have discussed the organization of the Apple II's graphics memory and developed some routines to draw points and lines, erase the screen, and perform some simple special effects. We now set our sights a little higher. How do we go about developing graphics routines that would be useful for animation?

Ultimate Speed

Before beginning our quest for animation-caliber graphics routines, we must clarify our needs. It should be obvious that one of the most important goals must be speed. The faster we can draw shapes on the screen, the longer we can spend calculating trajectories, collisions, and bookkeeping while still maintaining smooth, flicker-free motion.

Another feature of the finished routines should be flexibility. We may be willing to sacrifice a bit of speed if the graphics routines we develop can handle all of our shape-drawing needs. In addition, we'll continue to strive toward keeping our routines compact so more of the Apple's memory can be devoted to the graphics application.

Shape-Drawing Algorithms

One way to draw a shape on a graphics device is to develop an algorithm for drawing that shape. This is how lines, circles, rectangles and other simple shapes are drawn. We have even implemented some shape-drawing algorithms in previous sections.

The shape-drawing facility provided in Applesoft is an algorithm that unpacks shape descriptions (shape tables) and draws them by executing the appropriate sequence of "move" and "draw line" instructions. One advantage of this method is that the shapes can be stored in a relatively compact form. Also, since the shape is composed entirely of vectors, the shape can be scaled or rotated easily. The disadvantages are that a shape can be just one color, and the drawing process is slow. Because of speed considerations, we must come up with something better.

Bitblts

A very common operation in computer graphics copying data values from one location in memory to another, potentially displayable, area. This is called a "bitblt," or bit block transfer operation. Many processors provide a special instruction for moving blocks of memory around.

This block transfer instruction can be used to draw shapes on the screen quickly and efficiently. A shape is stored in some area of memory that is not being displayed and the bitbit operation is used to quickly copy it into memory that is being displayed. The shape can be a rectangle of any size and potentially be any data values (colors) that are allowed. This type of shape has been used often in games on the Apple II and is sometimes referred to as a 'block shape'.

Because the Apple's 6502 processor has no block transfer instruction, we'll have to develop a machine language routine to simulate it. This bitblt routine will form the basis for our shape-drawing routines. Since the bitblt operation is essentially a memory copy, we will be copying bytes of data from our shape table to the graphics memory of the Apple. Obviously our shapes will take up more space this way, but we will be able to draw them rapidly. We will have some problems because of the Apple's graphics memory organization.

Recall that information about seven pixels plus a color flag is stored in each byte of the Apple's graphics memory. Our shapes will have to contain the exact data values needed to display seven pixels on the screen in the fashion desired.

Home Movies

We wish to animate an object across the screen. As it moves, we'd like to show its legs moving, its antennae wobbling and its eyes rolling about in their sockets. Ideally, we'd like to develop an animation sequence-a series of still frames, that when displayed quickly enough in sequential locations on the screen, promotes the illusion of motion. In theory, this sequence could be as long as desired enough frames to complete the desired animation cycle. The cycle could be repeated many times as the shape moved about on the screen in any direction.

How do we do this on the Apple? Once we have defined a shape, we can move it vertically on the screen with no problem. We'll designate the upper left corner of the shape as the origin of the shape. Simply changing the y-coordinate of the origin will cause it to be drawn at any vertical location. We should be able to use our YTABLE to efficiently calculate the addresses in memory where the shape is to be drawn. We could even define an animation sequence of any number of frames, and select each of these frames in turn as the object is moved vertically up or down on the screen.

Things become confusing when we discuss horizontal motion. Suppose we restrict ourselves to byte boundaries in selecting the horizontal position on the screen. Our mouths drop open in disbelief when our shape comes out in different colors, depending on whether the starting byte address was even or odd! To see that this is so, try this: type HGR from Applesoft followed by a POKE 8192,85 and a POKE 8193,85. You POKEd the same value into two consecutive bytes of memory, but in the first case it came out green and in the second case it came out violet!

This is the nature of the beast we must deal with. One possible solution to this problem would be to require shapes to begin on even byte boundaries. This restriction, however, will not promote flicker-free graphics, so we must find ways to make it palatable.

One thing we can do is provide several versions of a particular shape, each shifted horizontally by a certain amount. The block shape itself will begin on an even byte boundary, but pixel data within the block may be shifted horizontally. Because of the even/odd column dilemma, let's make that "certain amount" be two pixels. This will assure that the shape will remain a constant color as it is shifted horizontally. Because of our earlier discussion, we know that a given shape will appear exactly the same if it is moved over two bytes. We therefore need only to take care of shifting a shape through two bytes. Two bytes equals 14 pixels and since we will shift by two pixels each time, we'll need seven different frames for the animation sequence.

Pixels shifted out of one byte must be shifted into the adjacent byte. The color flag (high bit) of each byte must also be maintained. It is clear that shifting pixels in and out of the data bytes on the fly will be time-consuming. We'll have to settle for shifting the shapes ahead of time and storing the dIfferent pre-shifted shapes in our shape table. Then, to draw our shape at 0,0 we'd use frame #1 of the sequence.

To draw it at 0,2 we'd use frame #2 at 0,4 we'd use frame #3, and so on. When we got to 0,14 we'd shift our starting horizontal position over two bytes and use frame #0 again.

This all sounds pretty confusing! Instead of one shape, we need seven. We can specify any value for the y-coordinate, but we can only use x-coordinates that fall on the left boundary of even numbered bytes! Have no fear! We'll develop our shape-drawing routines so that the proper frame of the seven in the sequence will be chosen automatically, and given a shape and an x and y coordinate on the Apple's screen. This discussion will help you to understand why shapes must be the way they are, and why our shape-drawing routines operate as they do.

The Shape Table

Making our shape tables completely relocatable is another must. This will allow us to put shape tables anywhere in memory and to have multiple shape tables in memory. We'll utilize the same page zero locations to point to our current shape table as Applesoft uses. We can then place the table anywhere in memory since we'll always have a pointer to it in a fixed location.

We'll start the shape table by allocating space for an offset to the next available byte of memory following the shape table. This way we can add shapes to existing tables. The number of shapes supported by the table must also be provided. We'll use offsets to shapes and to frames within shapes so that the tables remain completely relocatable, yet we can get to the start of any frame of any shape quickly.

Making Shapes

We'll look at a fairly simple Applesoft program that will let you turn shapes on the hi-res screen into an "animation shape table" of the type we've been discussing. This program will let you specify a rectangular region of the screen and will automatically expand it to the nearest whole byte boundary and compute the six additional shifted shapes.

The shape table generator program is shown in Listing 5.1. I call this program "MAT" for Make Animation Tables. MAT lets you use the game paddles to define a region of the hi-res graphics screen to turn into a shape.

MAT starts out by poking a simple Applesoft shape table into memory. This shape table contains the cursor shapes to be used in defining the region of a shape. Hi-res graphics are turned on without erasing the current contents of the screen. Next, an array is computed that contains the address of the first byte of every row in hi-res graphics memory page one. This array will act as a look-up table and speed up calculations which compute the shifted shapes.

When you enter the program, you'll be asked if you'll be using an old table. If you respond affirmatively, you will be prompted for the name of the shape table and it will be loaded from the disk. If not, a new shape table will be created in memory and you will be asked for a maximum number of shapes that the table may contain.

There are five main options available. If you enter the program with something on the hi-res screen, select the first option and adjust the cursors using the game paddles. Use the knobs to adjust the horizontal and vertical position of one of the cursors. Press one of the pushbuttons to switch to the other cursor. When the shape has been defined by using the paddles, press a key to return to the menu. In general you'll want to leave two bytes (14 pixels) to the right of the shape to allow room for the shifted shapes.

Once the shape boundaries have been adjusted using the paddles you can select option #2 to compute the shape and its shifted versions and add them to the shape table. If you want, you can use option #3 to load a hi-res screen that's been saved on disk to provide more shape-making material. You can use option #4 at any time to save the shape table on the disk.

Option #5 can be used once you become adept at making shape tables. It allows you to create shapes a single frame at a time. You must take care of the shifting yourself by positioning the object and the cursors properly. This allows you to add extra motion such as swinging arms, rolling eyes or changing colors to the animation sequence.

Listing 5.1 - Make Animation Tables Program

```
90   REM   MAKE ANIMATION TABLES
91   REM
92   REM     BY RANDI J. ROST
93   REM          3/30/83
100  REM
101  REM *****   INITIALIZATION   *****
105  DIM Y(192)
110  FOR I = 768 TO 794
120  READ SHAPE: POKE I,SHAPE: NEXT I
130  DATA  2,0,9,0,18,0,26,0,0,45,45,45,222,219
135  DATA  51,54,6,0,63,63,63,76,73,33,36,4,0
140  POKE 232,0: POKE 233,3
150  ROT= 0: SCALE= 1
160  HOME : VTAB 22
170  POKE  - 16297,0: POKE  - 16304,0
175  POKE  - 16301,0: POKE 33,40
180  FOR I = 0 TO 191
185 T0 =  INT (I / 8)
186 T0 = T0 -  INT (T0 / 8) * 8
190 T1 = I -  INT (I / 8) * 8
200 T2 =  INT (T0 / 8)
210 Y(I) = 8192 + T1 * 1024 + T0 * 128 + T2 * 40
220  NEXT I
490  HOME : VTAB 24
500  INPUT "WILL YOU BE USING AN OLD TABLE?";A$
510  IF  LEFT$ (A$,1) = "Y" THEN 700
520 START = 16384
525  HOME : VTAB 24
530  INPUT "INPUT MAX # OF SHAPES FOR TABLE?";NUM
540  POKE START + 2,NUM + 128
550  FOR I = START + 3 TO START + 2 + 2 * NUM: POKE I,0: NEXT
I
560 AVAIL = I: GOTO 900
```

48

```
700  INPUT "TYPE IN NAME OF OLD TABLE?";N$
710  PRINT  CHR$ (4);"BLOAD ";N$
720 START =  PEEK (43634) + 256 *  PEEK (43635)
730 AVAIL =  PEEK (START) + 256 *  PEEK (START + 1) + START
900  REM *****   MAIN MENU   *****
1000  HOME : VTAB 24
1010  PRINT "1) ADJUST CURSORS  2) GENERATE SHAPE"
1020  PRINT "3) LOAD HGR SCREEN 4) SAVE TABLE"
1025  PRINT "5) GENERATE A SINGLE FRAME OF A SHAPE"
1030  INPUT "ENTER WHICH?";A$
1040 T =  VAL (A$)
1045  PRINT
1050  ON T GOSUB 9000,8000,7000,6000,5000
1060  GOTO 1000
5000  REM *****   GENERATE A FRAME   *****
5008  HOME : VTAB 22
5010  INPUT "WHICH SHAPE NUMBER WILL THIS BE?";SN
5020 A1 = START + SN * 2 + 1
5030 T1 =  PEEK (A1):T2 =  PEEK (A1 + 1)
5040  IF T1 <  > 0 OR T2 <  > 0 THEN 5100
5050 T = AVAIL - A1
5060  POKE A1,T -  INT (T / 256) * 256: POKE A1 + 1, INT (T /
256)
5070 WIDTH =  INT ((X2 - X1) / 7) + 1: POKE AVAIL,WIDTH
5080 HEIGHT = Y2 - Y1 + 1: POKE AVAIL + 1,HEIGHT
5085 AVAIL = AVAIL + 2
5090  FOR I = AVAIL TO AVAIL + 13: POKE I,0: NEXT I:A1 =
AVAIL:AVAIL = I: GOTO 5200
5100 A1 = A1 + T1 + T2 * 256:WIDTH =  PEEK (A1):HEIGHT =  PEEK
(A1 + 1):A1 = A1 + 2
5200  INPUT "WHICH SEQ # WILL THIS BE?";SEQ
5210 T = A1 + (SEQ - 1) * 2
5220 T3 = AVAIL - T:T1 = T3 -  INT (T3 / 256) * 256:T2 =  INT
(T3 / 256)
5230  POKE T,T1: POKE T + 1,T2
5240  FOR I = Y1 TO Y1 + HEIGHT - 1
5250  FOR J =  INT (X1 / 7) TO  INT (X1 / 7) + WIDTH - 1
5260 T =  PEEK (Y(I) + J)
5270  POKE AVAIL,T
5280 AVAIL = AVAIL + 1
5290  NEXT J,I
5300  RETURN
6000  REM *****   SAVE SHAPE TABLE   *****
6010 T = AVAIL - START
```

```
6030  POKE START,T -  INT (T / 256) * 256: POKE START + 1, INT
(T / 256)
6035  HOME : VTAB 22
6040  INPUT "INPUT NAME FOR TABLE?";N$
6050  PRINT  CHR$ (4);"BSAVE ";N$;",A";START;",L";AVAIL -
START + 2
6060  RETURN
7000  REM *****   LOAD HI-RES SCREEN   *****
7005  HOME : VTAB 22
7010  INPUT "INPUT NAME OF SCREEN TO LOAD?";N$
7020  PRINT  CHR$ (4);"BLOAD ";N$;",A$2000"
7030  RETURN
8000  REM *****   GENERATE ENTIRE SHAPE SEQUENCE   *****
8010  HOME : VTAB 22
8020  INPUT "WHICH SHAPE NUMBER WILL THIS BE?";SN
8030 A1 = START + SN * 2 + 1
8040 T1 =  PEEK (A1):T2 =  PEEK (A1 + 1)
8050  IF T1 <  > 0 OR T2 <  > 0 THEN  PRINT "SHAPE ALREADY
DEFINED...": GOTO 8020
8060 T = AVAIL - A1
8070  POKE A1,T -  INT (T / 256) * 256: POKE A1 + 1, INT (T /
256)
8080 WIDTH =  INT ((X2 - X1) / 7) + 1: POKE AVAIL,WIDTH
8090 HEIGHT = Y2 - Y1 + 1: POKE AVAIL + 1,HEIGHT
8100 AVAIL = AVAIL + 2
8110 B(1) = AVAIL + 14
8120  FOR I = 1 TO 7
8130 T = B(I) - AVAIL
8140  POKE AVAIL,T -  INT (T / 256) * 256: POKE AVAIL + 1, INT
(T / 256)
8150 AVAIL = AVAIL + 2
8160 B(I + 1) = B(I) + HEIGHT * WIDTH
8170  NEXT I
8180 X3 =  INT (X1 / 7)
8190  FOR I = Y1 TO Y2
8200  FOR J = X3 TO X3 + WIDTH - 1
8210 T =  PEEK (Y(I) + J)
8230  POKE AVAIL,T
8240 AVAIL = AVAIL + 1
8250  NEXT J,I
8260  FOR I = 2 TO 7
8270  FOR J = 0 TO HEIGHT - 1
8280 FLAG = 0:RMDR = 0
8290  FOR K = B(I - 1) + J * WIDTH TO B(I - 1) + J * WIDTH +
WIDTH - 1
```

```
8300 T =  PEEK (K)
8310  IF T > 127 THEN T = T - 128:FLAG = 1
8320 T1 = T * 4 -  INT ((T * 4) / 128) * 128
8330 T2 =  INT ((T * 4) / 128)
8340 T1 = T1 + RMDR
8350 RMDR = T2
8360  IF FLAG = 1 THEN T1 = T1 + 128
8370  POKE AVAIL,T1
8380 AVAIL = AVAIL + 1
8390  NEXT K,J,I
8400  RETURN
9000  REM *****   ADJUST CURSORS   *****
9010 T = 0: HOME
9011 X1 =  INT ( PDL (0) * 279 / 255):X2 = X1 + 6: IF X2 > 279
THEN X2 = 279
9012 Y1 =  INT ( PDL (1) * 191 / 255):Y2 = Y1
9015 X7 = X1:Y7 = Y1:X8 = X2:Y8 = Y2
9020  XDRAW 1 AT X1,Y1
9030  XDRAW 2 AT X2,Y2
9040  IF  PEEK ( - 16287) > 127 THEN T =  NOT T
9050  IF  PEEK ( - 16286) > 127 THEN T =  NOT T
9060  IF  PEEK ( - 16384) > 127 THEN  POKE  - 16368,0: XDRAW 1
AT X1,Y1: XDRAW 2 AT X2,Y2: RETURN
9070  IF T THEN X4 =  PDL (0):Y4 =  PDL (1)
9080  IF  NOT T THEN X5 =  PDL (0):Y5 =  PDL (1)
9085 X1 =  INT (X4 * 279 / 255):X2 =  INT (X5 * 279 / 255)
9086 Y1 =  INT (Y4 * 191 / 255):Y2 =  INT (Y5 * 191 / 255)
9090 T1$ = " ":T2$ = " "
9100 X1 =  INT (X1 / 7) * 7
9110 X2 =  INT (X2 / 7) * 7 + 6
9112  IF X2 > 279 THEN X2 = 279
9120  VTAB 22: PRINT "X1=";X1;"  ";T1$;: HTAB 15: PRINT
"Y1=";Y1;"   "
9130  PRINT "X2=";X2;"  ";T2$;: HTAB 15: PRINT "Y2=";Y2;"   "
9135  IF X7 <  > X1 OR Y7 <  > Y1 THEN  XDRAW 1 AT X7,Y7:X7 =
X1:Y7 = Y1: XDRAW 1 AT X1,Y1
9140  IF X8 <  > X2 OR Y8 <  > Y2 THEN  XDRAW 2 AT X8,Y8:X8 =
X2:Y8 = Y2: XDRAW 2 AT X2,Y2
9145  GOTO 9040
```

A Finished Product

Listing 5.2 is a hex dump of a shape table created by MAT. The shape is a white rectangle (HCOLOR= 3) from 0,0 to 6,7. Let's take a close look at the values in the shape table in order to see exactly how it's organized.

The first two bytes are the offset to the next available memory location. Adding the offset ($00CF) to the start of the table ($6000) gives us the address $60CF which contains a zero. If we choose to add shapes to this table later on, the next one will start at location $60CF.

The next byte contains the number of shapes in the table. In addition the high bit of this byte is set so that this type of shape table can be distinguished from another, very similar shape table that we'll be discussing later on in this series. The number of shapes is never needed by the machine language routines, only (potentially) by utility programs that create, edit, copy, and merge these tables. In this case, the shape table contains space for ten shapes, and the high bit of this byte set to one uniquely identifies this as an animation shape table.

Adding three to the start address of the shape table gets us to the offset for the first shape in the table. This is also a two-byte offset, in this case $0014. Adding this offset to the current address ($6003) gives us the address ($6017) of the actual data for shape #1. Following the two-byte offset for shape #1 are nine pairs of zero bytes, indicating that shapes 2-10 are currently undefined.

Starting at location $6017 we see two bytes that indicate that this shape is 3 bytes wide and 8 pixels high. Seven sets of 2-byte offset follow, These are used in accessing each of the seven frames of the shape. Since shapes can be any height and width, we'll avoid any time-consuming multiplications by storing the offsets to the data for each frame. A simple addition of the offset and the current address gets us to the data for the desired frame.

For instance, assume we decide to draw frame #4 of shape #1. We get to location $601F and find our offset to be $0050. A simple addition leads us to the shape data which begins at location $606F. At that address we'll find eight sets of bytes that read "40 3F 00" corresponding to our original rectangle shape shifted over by six bits.

Listing 5.2 - Shape Table Hex Dump

```
*6000.60CF
6000- CF 00 8A 14 00 00 00 00
6008- 00 00 00 00 00 00 00 00
6010- 00 00 00 00 00 00 00 03
6018- 08 0E 00 24 00 3A 00 50
6020- 00 66 00 7C 00 92 00 7F
6028- 00 00 7F 00 00 7F 00 00
6030- 7F 00 00 7F 00 00 7F 00
6038- 00 7F 00 00 7F 00 00 7C
6040- 03 00 7C 03 00 7C 03 00
6048- 7C 03 00 7C 03 00 7C 03
6050- 00 7C 03 00 7C 03 00 70
6058- 0F 00 70 0F 00 70 0F 00
6060- 70 0F 00 70 0F 00 70 0F
6068- 00 70 0F 00 70 0F 00 40
6070- 3F 00 40 3F 00 40 3F 00
6078- 40 3F 00 40 3F 00 40 3F
6080- 00 40 3F 00 40 3F 00 00
6088- 7E 01 00 7E 01 00 7E 01
6090- 00 7E 01 00 7E 01 00 7E
6098- 01 00 7E 01 00 7E 01 00
60A0- 78 07 00 78 07 00 78 07
60A8- 00 78 07 00 78 07 00 78
60B0- 07 00 78 07 00 78 07 00
60B8- 60 1F 00 60 1F 00 60 1F
60C0- 00 60 1F 00 60 1F 00 60
60C8- 1F 00 60 1F 00 60 1F 00
*
```

Making Your Own Shapes

For practice, try using the MAT program to create a shape table identical to that found in Listing 5.2. Write a little program that will draw a box with HCOLOR=3 from 0,0 to 6,7. Run the program to draw the box on the screen and then run the program MAT.

You'll want to create a new shape table, so answer with "N" when asked if you'll be using an old table. Type 10 for the number of shapes this table will hold. Select the "ADJUST CURSOR" option from the menu and use the paddles to set xl=O, yl=O, x2=20, and y2

53

= 7. Press any key to get back to the main menu. Select the "GENERATE SHAPE" option and make this shape number one.

When the shape has been generated and the prompt returns, save the shape table to disk and use a ctrl-C to exit the program. BLOAD your table into a suitable location in memory ($6000 is fine) and compare it to Listing 5.2. The values should be identical.

Next Time

The shape we have created here is not very exciting, but we have laid the groundwork for some powerful machine language subroutines for animation. In the next chapter, we'll take a look at the routines to draw shapes of the sort described in this chapter. Between now and then, use your imagination and your shape table generator program and create some interesting shapes. After next time you'll be able to animate any of the shapes you develop!

If you have become completely lost by this discussion, don't worry. After developing the machine language routine to draw these shapes, the reasons for our shape table structure should become clear. We'll develop the routine so that you only need to pass the shape number and the actual x and y coordinate at which it is to be drawn. All the dirty work will be handled by our shape table generator program and the assembly language drawing routines. Stay tuned!

CHAPTER 6

The development of a shape-making utility program in the last chapter has paved the way for this installment's topic-a machine-language routine for drawing block shapes. Chapter 5 discussed the goals of our shape-drawing efforts and the motivation for the design of the shape table. Go back and reread that if it's still a little fuzzy. Use the MAT program to make a shape of your own, because now we're going to animate it!

Algorithm Overview

The algorithm presented here to draw block shapes is actually fairly trivial. The 6502's 8-bit arithmetic and the Apple's complicated graphics memory organization work together to bury the algorithm under a mountain of unpleasant details. For that reason, we'll first look at the high-level algorithm. Then we'll discuss the implementation details as we go through the shape-drawing routine line by line.

The shape-drawing routine will expect three input values: x-position (high and low bytes), y-position, and the number of the shape to be drawn. The first step is to calculate a pointer to the shape data, given only the shape number and a pointer to the start of the shape table. We'll adopt the convention that the first shape in the table will be referred to as shape #1 and not shape #0.

You'll recall that the shape table starts with a byte containing the number of shapes in the table, two bytes representing an offset to the next available memory location, and then a series of two-byte offsets to shapes, one for each shape in the table. We can calculate a pointer to the offset for shape n by adding 2*n + 1 to the starting address of the shape table. This offset will be read and added to the current pointer value, resulting in a pointer to the first byte of shape data for shape #no.

Now recall that each shape contains a width (in bytes), a height (in pixels), two-byte offsets for each of the seven frames in the shape, and then the actual data for each of the seven frames. The width and height will be used as the loop boundaries for a two-dimensional transfer loop.

55

We must now calculate the frame number of the shape that should be used, given the x-coordinate where the shape is to be drawn. For x=0 or 1, we should use frame #1, for x=2 or 3 we'll use frame #2, and so on until we get to frame #7 when x = 12 or 13. For x = 14 or 15, we'll use frame #1 again, moved over two bytes. The formula for the frame number to use is FRAME = (X/2) MOD 7 + 1. Funny thing. Way back in Chapter 1, we included a lookup table to compute MOD 7 values! At last we get to use it!

Once we have computed which frame to use, we can multiply the frame number by two and add the result to our pointer. This leaves us pointing at the two-byte offset for the desired frame. We can add this two-byte offset to the pointer to arrive at the start of the actual data for the desired frame.

The rest is easy. We simply set up a nested loop to transfer data from rows and columns in our shape table to rows and columns on the graphics screen.

Implementation Details

Listing 6.1 shows the machine-language implementation of the algorithm discussed above. Let's examine some of the gory details.

The first thing you might notice is that the routine has two entry points. This allows the routine to serve two purposes. Sometimes we'll want to replace whatever is on the screen with data from the shape table. This is what happens when the DRAW entry point is used. Other times we'll want to exclusive-or the shape data with whatever is on the screen. The XDRAW entry point can be used to do this. XDRAWing a shape a second time in the same position will erase it, leaving the screen contents unaffected.

The first order of business for both DRAW and XDRAW is to store the registers away for later use. Then, in each case, the controversial, but sometimes useful technique of self-modifying code is used to "create" the difference between DRAW and XDRAW. The only difference between the two routines is that XDRAW requires an extra instruction in the actual transfer loop to exclusive-or the current contents of the screen with the shape data before storing the result to the screen. The XDRAW entry point causes the 6502 EOR instruction to be stored at the appropriate location in the transfer loop, and the DRAW entry point causes two Nap instructions to be stored there. Actually, there are two such transfer loops that must be modified. The second one will appear in a subroutine to draw shapes that are only partially within the graphics window in the next chapter.

What are the advantages of self-modifying code in this case? We saved a few bytes of storage and perhaps made our transfer loop an instruction or two shorter (faster). The price? We made the source code more difficult to understand, we ruled out the possibility of ROM implementations, and debugging is harder. Since the routine is already debugged (I hope!), only the first two are issues. Oh well. Here, speed and compactness are more desirable than understandability when a choice has to be made.

The routine now proceeds to build up a pointer to the shape data in the sequence described above. Lines 65-68 compute SHAPE*2+1, and this value is added to the pointer in lines 69-76. Next the offset to the desired shape is read and added to the pointer (lines 77-83), giving us a pointer to the start of the desired shape definition.

The width and height of the shape are now read and stored for later use. We can now determine whether any portion of the shape is outside the current graphics window. If so, we'll jump to the routine DRAWPART. For now, DRAWPART is simply a return so that no shape will be drawn unless it is entirely within the window.

I also wanted to be able to specify negative values for X and Y so that shapes can be scrolled completely off the screen. For Y, I decided that values of 0-191 would indicate positive Y values and values from 192 to 255 would be used to represent Y values from -64 to -1. X-coordinates with a high-byte of $FF will also be interpreted as negative values. For instance, passing the values $FE, $FF, and $FE in the Y, A, and X registers will cause the shape to be drawn at the location (-2, -2).

Lines 92-142 check all the possibilities. If either X or Y is negative, if X is less than the left window edge or X+WIDTH is greater than the right window edge, or if Y is less than the window top or Y + HEIGHT is greater than the window bottom, we'll jump to the routine to draw a partially visible shape. If we arrive at line 143, the shape must be completely visible.

Lines 143-170 calculate the frame number that should be used. This is accomplished using the XMODTBL, but is complicated by the fact that the XMODTBL spans two pages of memory. Sometimes it's necessary to access values in that second page, but we don't want to modify the pointer to the XMODTBL. Solution: copy the pointer to another location and increment it there if necessary.

Once the frame number has been computed, lines 171-186 finish computing the pointer to the actual frame data to be used.

So far we've done nothing but set-up work for the main loop! The remaining 30 or so lines actually do the work. For each row, the x counter is initialized to the width of the shape and the address of the first screen byte to be affected is computed. For each byte within the row, a byte of shape data is read, the appropriate action (EOR or NOP) is taken, the result stored back in hi-res memory, and the pointers and counters updated.

Well that's it! It's more important that you understand the general algorithm and the shape table structure than every line of assembly code in Listing 6.1. If you understand the basic algorithm and some of the considerations, you can write similar routines on other computers and in other languages.

Listing 6.1 - Block Shape Routines

```
*
* DRAW AND XDRAW ARE USED TO DRAW ANIMATION (BLOCK)
* SHAPES. MAKE SURE SHPTABL CONTAINS A POINTER TO
* A VALID SHAPE TABLE AND PASS THE NUMBER OF THE
* SHAPE TO BE DRAWN IN $09 AND THE POSITION OF THE
* UPPER LEFT CORNER OF THE SHAPE IN THE REGISTERS
* WITH XLO IN X, XHI IN A AND Y IN THE Y REGISTER. DRAW
* CAUSES SHAPE DATA TO OVERWRITE THE CONTENTS OF HI-RES
* MEMORY XDRAW EXCLUSIVE OR'S SHAPE DATA WITH THE
* CONTENTS OF SCREEN MEMORY - XDRAWING A SHAPE WILL
* DISPLAY IT. XDRAWING IT AGAIN WILL ERASE IT, LEAVING
* THE HI-RES SCREEN UNAFFECTED.
*
            ORG     $AFE
XLOCLO      EQU     $06
XLOCHI      EQU     $07
YLOC        EQU     $08
SHPNO       EQU     $09
HGADRLO     EQU     $1E
HGADRHI     EQU     $1F
```

```
HGPRG       EQU    $E6
YTABL       EQU    $EC
YATBH       EQU    $EE
SHPTABL     EQU    $FA
SHPBASL     EQU    $FC
SHPBASH     EQU    $FD
FRMBASL     EQU    $D4
FRMBASH     EQU    $D5
XDIVTBL     EQU    $4C
XMODTBL     EQU    $D0
TEMPPTR2    EQU    $D2
WNDWTOP     EQU    $A6A
WNDWBOT     EQU    $A6B
WNDWRLO     EQU    $A6C
WNDWRHI     EQU    $A6D
WNDWLLO     EQU    $A6E
WNDWLHI     EQU    $A6F
DEORLOC2    EQU    $D8C
XBYTE  DS   1
XDIV2  DS   1
HEIGHT DS   1
WIDTH  DS   1
DTEMPX DS   1
DTEMPY DS   1
BOTTOMY     DS     1


STOREREG    STA    XLOCHI
       STX    XLOCLO
       STY    YLOC
       RTS


DRAW   JSR    STOREREG    ;SAVE SHAPE POSITION FOR LATER
       LDA    #$EA
       STA    DEORLOC     ;STORE NOPS IF
       STA    DEORLOC+1   ;DRAW ENTRY PT USED
       STA    DEORLOC2
       STA    DEORLOC2+1
       BMI    DSTART


XDRAW  JSR    STOREREG
       LDA    #$51
       STA    DEORLOC     ;STORE EOR IF XDRAW
       STA    DEORLOC2    ;ENTRY PT IS USED
       LDA    #$1E
       STA    DEORLOC+1
```

59

```
        STA     DEORLOC2+1

DSTART LDA      SHPNO   ;LOAD THE SHAPE NUMBER
       ASL              ;MULTIPLY BY 2
       TAY              ;STORE IN Y
       INY              ;ADD 1
       TYA
       CLC
       ADC      (SHPTABL),Y  ;LOAD SHAPE OFFSET LO
       STA      SHPBASL      ;STORE IT IN SHAPE BASE PTR
       INY
       LDA      (SHPTABL),Y  ;LOAD SHAPE OFFSET HI
       ADC      SHPTABL+1    ;ADD START ADR HI OF TABLE
       STA      SHPBASH      ;STORE SHAPE BASE ADR HI
       CLC
       LDA      SHPBASL      ;LOAD SHAPE OFFSET LO
       ADC      SHPTABL      ;ADD START ADR LO
       STA      SHPBASL      ;STORE SHAPE BASE ADR LO
       LDA      #$00   ;ADD CARRY
       ADC      SHPBASH      ;TO HIGH BYTE
       STA      SHPBASH
       LDY      #$00
       LDA      (SHPBASL),Y  ;GET SHAPE WIDTH
       STA      WIDTH
       INY
       LDA      (SHPBASL),Y  ;GET SHAPE HEIGHT
       STA      HEIGHT

* CHECK TO SEE IF ANY PART OF SHAPE
* WILL BE OFF THE PRE-DEFINED WINDOW

       CLC              ;CHECK IF SHAPE EXCEEDS
       LDA      YLOC    ;TOP OF WINDOW. IF
       CMP      #$C0    ;SEE IF Y<0
       BLT      CONT0
       JMP      DRAWPART

CONT0  CMP      WNDWTOP      ;YLOC >= WNDWTOP THEN
       BGE      CONT1   ;CONTINUE CHECK,
       JMP      DRAWPART     ;ELSE JUMP TO PARTIAL DRAW

CONT1  CLC
       ADC      HEIGHT ;CHECK IF SHAPE EXCEEDS
       CMP      WNDWBOT      ;BOTTOM OF WINDOW. IF
       BEQ      CONT1B ;YLOC+HEIGHT <=WNDWBOT
```

```
         BLT     CONT1B ;THEN CONTINUE CHECK
         JMP     DRAWPART      ;ELSE JUMP TO PARTIAL DRAW


CONT1B LDA      XLOCHI
         CMP     #$FF   ;IF XHI = -1, SHP IS OFFSCREEN
         BNE     CONT2
         JMP     DRAWPART      ;JUMP TO PARTIAL DRAW


CONT2  LDA      XLOCLO
         STA     TEMPPTR2      ;STORE X'S FOR FUTURE USE
         LDA     XLOCHI
         STA     TEMPPTR2+1    ;CHECK IF SHAPE EXCEEDS
         CMP     WNDWLHI       ;LEFT EDGE. IF XLOCHI=WNDWLHI
         BEQ     CONT3  ;WE MUST CHECK LO BYTE.
         BGE     CONT4  ;IF XLOCHI>WNDWLHI, CONT.
         JMP     DRAWPART      ;ELSE JUMP TO PARTIAL DRAW


CONT3  LDA      XLOCLO ;CHECK LEFT EDGE BYTE
         CMP     WNDWLLO       ;COORD WHEN HI BYTES =
         BGE     CONT4  ;CONTINUE IF XLOCLO>=WNDWLLO
         JMP     DRAWPART      ;ELSE JUMP TO PARTIAL DRAW


CONT4  LDA      WIDTH  ;ADD WIDTH TO LEFT
         ASL            ;EDGE COORDINATE
         ASL            ;(WIDTH IS IN BYTES, SO MUST
         ASL
         CLC            ;MULTIPLY BY 8 TO GET WIDTH IN PIXELS)
         ADC     TEMPPTR2      ;STORE COMPUTED RIGHT EDGE
         STA     TEMPPTR2      ;(IN PIXELS) IN TEMPPTR2
         BCC     CONT5
         INC     TEMPPTR2+1


CONT5  CLC
         LDA     TEMPPTR2+1    ;CHECK IF SHAPE EXCEEDS
         CMP     WNDWRHI       ;RIGHT EDGE
         BEQ     CONT6  ;BR TO CONT6 IF XRTHI=WNDWRHI
         BLT     CONT7  ;IF XRTHI<WNDWRHI CONTINUE
         JMP     DRAWPART      ;ELSE JUMP TO PARTIAL DRAW


CONT6  LDA      TEMPPTR2      ;CHECK LO BYTES WHEN HI ARE =
         CMP     WNDWRLO       ;IF XRTLO<=WNDWRLO, SHAPE
         BEQ     CONT7  ;IS WITHIN WINDOW
         BLT     CONT7
         JMP     DRAWPART      ;ELSE JUMP TO PARTIAL DRAW
```

```
CONT7  LDA    XDIVTBL
       STA    TEMPPTR2      ;GET PTRS TO X/7 TABLE
       LDA    XDIVTBL+1
       STA    TEMPPTR2+1
       LDA    XLOCHI ;IF X>255
       BEQ    LT256A3       ;INCREMENT TEMPPTR

LT256A3       LDY    XLOCLO ;LOAD INDEX TO TABLE
       LDA    (TEMPPTR2),Y ;LOAD VALUE FOR X/7
       LSR                 ;MAKE SURE WE HAVE
       ASL                 ;AN EVEN-NUMBERED BYTE
       STA    XBYTE ;STORE RESULT IN XBYTE
       LDA    XMODTBL
       STA    TEMPPTR2      ;GET PTRS TO
       LDA    XMODTBL+1     ;(X MOD 7) + 1 TABLE
       STA    TEMPPTR2+1
       LDA    XLOCLO ;DIVIDE BY 2 TO GET RESOLUTION
       LSR                 ;IN THE RANGE 0-139
       STA    XDIV2
       LDA    XLOCHI ;ADD #$80 TO ABOVE RESULT IF
       CMP    #$00   ;HI PART EQUALS 1
       BEQ    LT256A5
       LDA    #$80

LT256A5       ADC    XDIV2
       TAY
       DEY                 ;NOW HAVE CORRECT INDEX TO XMODTBL
       LDA    (TEMPPTR2),Y ;LOAD VALUE FOR (X MOD 7)+1
       ASL                 ;MULTIPLY BY 2 TO GET
       TAY                 ;PROPER OFFSET FOR DESIRED FRAME
       CLC
       ADC    (SHPBASL),Y  ;ADD OFFSET FOR FRAME
       STA    FRMBASL       ;TO GET TOTAL OFFSET FOR FRAME
       INY
       LDA    (SHPBASL),Y  ;LOAD OFFSET HI
       ADC    SHPBASH       ;ADD HI BYTE OF SHP ADR
       STA    FRMBASH       ;STORE HI BYTE OF OFFSET TO FRAME
       CLC
       LDA    FRMBASL       ;LOAD LO BYTE OF OFFSET TO FRAME
       ADC    SHPBASL       ;ADD LO BYTE OF PTR TO SHP
       STA    FRMBASL       ;STORE LO BYTE OF FRAME PTR
       LDA    #$00   ;ADD CARRY
       ADC    FRMBASH       ;TO HIGH BYTE
       STA    FRMBASH
```

```
DRAWSHP      LDA    YLOC
        STA    DTEMPY ;SAVE STARTING Y FOR FUTURE REF
        ADC    HEIGHT ;COMPUTE BOTTOM LINE
        STA    BOTTOMY        ;THAT SHAPE WILL USE
        LDX    #$00

DLOOP1 LDA    WIDTH ;START OF TRANSFER LOOP
        STA    DTEMPX ;LOOP COUNTER FOR ONE ROW
        LDY    DTEMPY
        LDA    (YTABL),Y    ;GET LO PART OF ADRS
        CLC          ; OF LEFTMOST BYTE OF ROW
        ADC    XBYTE
        STA    HGADRLO
        LDA    #$00
        ADC    (YTABH),Y    ;DO SAME FOR HI BYTE
        ORA    HGRPG ;GET CORRECT HGRPG
        STA    HGADRHI        ;STORE COMPUTED HI BYTE OF ADRS
        LDY    #$00

DLOOP2 LDA    (FRMBASL,X)   ;LOAD NEXT BYTE OF SHAPE
DEORLOC        EOR    (HGADRLO),Y  ;EOR WITH WHAT'S ON SCREEN
        STA    (HGADRLO),Y  ;STORE RESULT BACK ON SCREEN
        CLC
        INC    HGADRLO       ;INC PTR TO NEXT
        BNE    DNOCAR ;SCREEN ADDRESS
        INC    HGADRHI

DNOCAR CLC
        INC    FRMBASL       ;INC PTR TO NEXT
        BNE    DNOCAR2       ;  BYTE OF SHAPE
        INC    FRMBASH

DNOCAR2      DEC    DTEMPX ;DEC BYTE COUNTER
        BNE    DLOOP2 ;IF ROW NOT DONE, LOOP BACK
        INC    DTEMPY ; ELSE INC ROW COUNTER
        LDA    DTEMPY
        CLC          ;CHECK IF LAST ROW
        CMP    BOTTOMY        ;HAS BEEN REACHED.
        BMI    DLOOP1 ;IF NOT, LOOP BACK FOR MORE
        RTS          ;ELSE ALL DONE!!!

DRAWPART     RTS          ;RETURN IF SHAPE IS PARTIALLY
OFFSCREEN
```

Demo Time

Listing 6.2 is a short demo program that can be used as your stepping-stone to animation greatness! First of all, BLOAD all the machine-language routines presented in Parts 1-4. Then BLOAD a valid shape table at the address $8800. You can use the simple shape table from Chapter 5 or use one of your own.

If you now BRUN the program in Listing 6.2, you will see shape #1 of the table scrolled from left to right across the screen. You can alter the delay loop to speed up or slow down the animation. You will probably see some "tearing" of the shape as it moves across the screen. This is caused when the phosphors of the monitor are updated (refreshed) by the electron gun at a time when the shape has been erased. We'll talk about a way to overcome this problem in a future installment.

In the next chapter we'll develop that routine to handle shapes that are only partially visible. Experiment with different shapes, and vary Y instead of (or in addition to) X in the demo program.

Listing 6.2 - Demo 6

```
*
*
            ORG     $6000
INIT        EQU     $803
XDRAW       EQU     $B1F
HGR         EQU     $865
SHPTABL     EQU     $FA
SHPNO       EQU     $09
XPOS        DS      1
YPOS        DS      1

DEMO6  LDA  #$1B    ;LOAD A WITH YTABLE ADR HI
       LDX  #$00    ; LOAD X WITH YTABLE ADR LO
       JSR  INIT    ;SET UP LOOKUP TABLE PTRS
       LDA  #$00    ;LOAD PTR TO SHAPE TABLE AT $8800
       STA  SHPTABL
       LDA  #$88
       STA  SHPTABL+1
```

```
        JSR   HGR     ;ENABLE HI-RES GRAPHICS PAGE #1
        LDA   #$01    ;WE'LL USE SHAPE #1 OF TABLE
        STA   SHPNO
        LDA   #$40    ;Y-COORDINATE WILL BE 64
        STA   YPOS
        LDA   #$00    ;X-COORDINATE STARTS AT 0
        STA   XPOS

LOOP    LDX   XPOS    ;LOAD UP REGISTERS TO
        LDA   #$00    ;   DRAW SHAPE AT CURRENT X,Y
        LDY   YPOS
        JSR   XDRAW   ;XDRAW THE SHAPE
        LDX   #$10    ;SLOW DOWN THE ANIMATION
        JSR   DELAY
        LDX   XPOS    ;XDRAW THE SHAPE A SECOND TIME
        LDA   #$00    ;   TIME TO ERASE IT
        LDY   YPOS
        JSR   XDRAW
        INC   XPOS    ;XPOS=XPOS+2
        INC   XPOS
        BNE   LOOP    ;LOOP UNTIL X=256(0)
        RTS

DELAY   LDY   #255
DELAY2  DEY
        BNE   DELAY2
        DEX
        BNE   DELAY
        RTS
```

CHAPTER 7

In the last chapter we developed a routine to display block shapes on the hires graphics screen. Due to space considerations, we left out a very important part of that routine-clipping the shape to the graphics window boundaries. Our routine could handle only shapes entirely within the graphics window. This time we'll extend the DRAW routine to display shapes that are only partially within the graphics window.

Clipping

Clipping, or the act of discarding all parts of an object outside a given boundary, is a fundamental problem in computer graphics. Several algorithms have been developed to clip lines to two-dimensional and three-dimensional rectangular boundaries. Algorithms have also been developed to clip arbitrary polygons to a rectangular boundary.

Our application makes use of a rectangular viewing area which we have called the graphics window. The graphics window is set by making calls to CHGUPLFT and CHGLOWRT. Now we'd like to be able to draw rectangular shapes in such a way that only the area within the graphics window is affected. Thus we need to clip rectangles against our rectangular boundary. In the following discussion, the location of the rectangular shape to be drawn is assumed to be the (x,y) pair at the shape's upper left corner. This point will be referred to as the position of the shape, and its position will be noted by X and Y.

The most simplistic algorithm we can conceive operates as follows. First, check the y-coordinate of each line of the shape before it is drawn. I f the y-coordinate is above the top of the graphics window or below the bottom of the window, skip the row entirely and go on to the next. Then, for each row not skipped, transfer only those pixels for which the x-coordinate is greater than or equal to the left edge of the window and less than or equal to the right edge.

Some improvements on the algorithm should be immediately obvious. First of all, the shape could be immediately rejected if it is found that Y is below the bottom of the window, since the entire shape must lie below the window. Similarly, if X is to the right of the right edge of the window, or if X+WIDTH is left of the left edge of the

67

window, or if Y + HEIGHT is above the top of the window, the shape can be rejected immediately.

In addition, simple arithmetic can be used to determine the first row or column of the shape that is visible. Just subtract the window boundary coordinate from X or Y. For example, to compute how many rows to skip for a shape at 10,10 when WINDOWTOP= 15, compute 15 10. This indicates that five rows of shape data should be skipped before starting.

These are some of the ideas we'll include in our rectangle-clipping algorithm. To save code space, the trivial reject cases won't be implemented. The philosophy for this is that the user should take advantage of the speed of the graphics routines and not be wasting time drawing a lot of shapes that are off the screen. In other words, the trivial reject cases are left to the user. They can be done empirically, by not calling the shape draw routines with shapes that are completely outside the graphics window, or they can be done by calling the shape draw routines and letting them go through a little extra work to see that the shape is totally outside the graphics window.

The Algorithm

Once again, a fairly straightforward algorithm will become quite clouded after taking into consideration the 6502 8-bit arithmetic and Apple graphics memory organization. For this reason, we will first describe the algorithm to draw partially visible shapes from a high level, then look at its implementation line by line.

By the time it is determined that a shape is only partly visible, the DRAW routine will have computed a pointer to the beginning of the data for the shape that is to be drawn. The first step of our algorithm is to compute the pointer to the start of data for the correct frame of the specified shape. This is done in the same fashion as it is done for DRAW. One complication is added by the fact that X may be negative and some extra steps are needed to calculate which frame to use in such a case.

Once the pointer to the actual shape data has been computed, we'll check to see if Y is above the top of the graphics window. If it is, we'll determine how many rows of shape data are above the window and skip past MIN(HEIGHT * WIDTH, (WINDOWTOP Y) * WIDTH) bytes of shape data. If Y is not above the top of the graphics window, we'll just start at the beginning of the shape data.

At this point, our CUITent y is equal to WINDOWTOP. Now for each row, perform the following steps:

1. See if current y is greater than WINDOWBOTTOM.
2. If it is, go to end since we are done drawing shape.
3. Otherwise.
   a. current x = X
   b. Skip past all shape table data bytes (if any) for which CUITent x is less than left of window
   c. Draw all bytes of data (if any) for which Current x is less than or equal to right of window
   d. Skip all bytes of shape data (if any) for which Current x is greater than right of window
   e. Increment current y
   f. If there is more shape data, goto step 1

Again, this algorithm will be somewhat slower in cases where a shape is entirely outside the window, but we've decided to leave it up to the programmer to make sure it doesn't happen very often.

Implementation

The routine shown in Listing 7.1 is the embodiment of the algorithm described above. For best results, include this routine in the same file as the DRAW routine presented in Chapter 6. Just skip over all the EQUs and DS's that are common to both routines and add the DRAWPART routine onto the end of the DRAW routine. After all, it is an integral part of the DRAW routine.

DRAWPART begins by computing the y value of the bottom row of the shape in lines 32-35. This value is stored in BOTTOMY for later use. Next, the routine finishes calculating the pointer to the actual shape frame data to be drawn. Lines 32-69 accomplish this in a manner nearly identical to lines 150-186 of the DRAW routine.

Lines 70-76 check to see if we need to skip any entire rows of data because of y values less than 0 or y values above the top of the graphics window. Lines 77-90 contain a loop that skips past these rows if necessary. When finished with the loop, if there is no more shape data to be read, we are done (lines 85·87).

When we've reached line 91, the Y-register contains the y value of the first potentially visible row of the shape, and FRMBASL and FRMBASH point to the first potentially visible byte of shape data. Lines 91-189 form a big loop that processes all remaining rows of the shape to be drawn.

The first step (lines 91-94) is to see whether the current y value is below the bottom of the window. If it is, we are done. Lines 95 and 96 set up the counter we'll use in our loop for all the bytes in the current row. Lines 97-128 handle skipping past all bytes in the row for which X is less than zero.

In lines 129-140, the first byte in the row to be (potentially) modified is computed using the XDIVTBL. When we reach SXCONT (line 141) the A register contains the number of the first byte in the row that may be overwritten with shape data, and TEMPCNT contains the number of bytes of data remaining for this row of the shape. (When TEMPCNT reaches 0, we're done with the row, no matter what we're doing.)

Lines 142-151 read past all shape data bytes for which the current x is less than the left edge of the window. Lines 152-176 form the loop for drawing any remaining visible bytes of the shape. Lines 177-182 read past any shape data bytes for which current x is greater than the right edge of the window. Lines 183-187 increment the row number and jump back to process any remaining rows of shape data.

Listing 7.1 - DRAWPART Routine

```
*
* DRAWPART IS A SUBROUTINE THAT IS CALLED BY DRAW OR
* XDRAW TO DRAW SHAPES THAT ARE ONLY PARTIALLY WITHIN
* THE GRAPHICS WINDOW. ALL PARTS OF THE SHAPE OUTSIDE
* THE WINDOW ARE CLIPPED.  WHAT REMAINS IS DRAWN.
*

        ORG     $C68
```

```
XLOCLO EQU    $06
XLOCHI EQU    $07
YLOC   EQU    $08
HGADRLO       EQU    $1E
HGADRHI       EQU    $1F
HGPRG  EQU    $E6
YTABL  EQU    $EC
YATBH  EQU    $EE
SHPBASL       EQU    $FC
SHPBASH       EQU    $FD
FRMBASL       EQU    $D4
FRMBASH       EQU    $D5
XDIVTBL       EQU    $4C
XMODTBL       EQU    $D0
TEMPPTR2      EQU    $D2
HEIGHT EQU    $B00
WIDTH  EQU    $B01
DTEMPX EQU    $B02
DTEMPY EQU    $B03
BOTTOMY       EQU    $B04
LFTXBYTE      EQU    $A68
RTXBYTE       EQU    $A69
WNDWTOP       EQU    $A6A
WNDWBOT       EQU    $A6B


DRAWPART      LDA    YLOC    ;COMPUTE BOTTOM COORD
       CLC                   ;OF SHAPE TO BE DRAWN
       ADC    HEIGHT
       STA    BOTTOMY
       LDA    XLOCLO ;DIVIDE X BY 2 TO GET HORIZ.
       LSR           ;  RESOLUTION IN RANGE 0-139
       STA    TXLO
       LDY    XLOCHI
       BEQ    GITXMOD        ;IF XHI-0, WE'RE READY FOR LOOKUP
       CPY    #$FF   ;IF XHI=-1, BRANCH TO NEGX
       BEQ    NEGX
       LDA    TXLO   ;XHI = 1, SO ADJUST TXLO
       ADC    #$02   ;  BY TWO TO GET PROPER INDEX
       STA    TXLO   ;  FOR LOOKUP TABLE
       BNE    GITXMOD

NEGX   CLC                   ;XHI=-1 SO ADJUST TXLO
       LDA    TXLO   ;  BY FIVE TO GET PROPER INDEX
       ADC    #$05   ;  FOR LOOKUP TABLE
       STA    TXLO
```

71

```
GITXMOD        LDY    TXLO
        LDA    (XMODTBL),Y  ;LOAD X MOD VALUE FROM TABLE
        ASL             ;MULTIPLY BY 2 TO GET PROPER
        TAY             ;  OFFSET TO DESIRED FRAME
        CLC
        ADC    (SHPBASL),Y  ;SET PROPER OFFSET TO ACTUAL
        STA    FRMBASL      ;   FRAME DATA
        INY
        LDA    (SHPBASL),Y
        ADC    SHPBASH      ;COMPUTE HI PART OF FRAME OFFSET
        STA    FRMBASH
        CLC
        LDA    SHPBASL      ;ADD OFFSET TO SHAPE TABLE
        ADC    FRMBASL      ;  PTR TO GET PTR TO FRAME DATA
        STA    FRMBASL
        LDA    #$00  ;COMPUTE HI PART OF PTR
        ADC    FRMBASH      ;  TO ACTUAL FRAME DATA
        STA    FRMBASH
        LDA    HEIGHT
        STA    TEMPCNT      ;TEMPCNT WILL BE # ROWS ONSCREEN
        LDY    YLOC   ;CHECK TO SEE IF -64 <Y<0
        CPY    #$C0   ;VALUES >$C0 INDICATE NEGATIVE Y'S
        BGE    SKIPROW      ;IF Y<0, MUST SKIP SOME ROWS
        CPY    WNDWTOP      ;IF Y<WNDWTOP, MUST SKIP ROWS
        BGE    SYOK   ;OTHERWISE, IT'S COOL

SKIPROW        LDA    HEIGHT ;KEEP TRACK OF ROWS REMAINING
        STA    TEMPCNT      ;   IN SHAPE IN TEMPCNT

SKIPLOOP       LDA    WIDTH  ;LOAD WIDTH OF SHAPE
        CLC
        ADC    FRMBASL      ;ADD WIDTH TO SHAPE FRAME
        STA    FRMBASL      ;   TO "SKIP" ONE ROW OF SHAPE DATA
        BCC    SLT256A
        INC    FRMBASH

SLT256A        DEC    TEMPCNT      ;DECREMENT REMAINING ROWS
        BNE    SCNT
        JMP    SDONE  ;SHAPE IS TOTALLY ABOVE WINDOW

SCNT    INY
        CPY    WNDWTOP      ;DOES Y=WNDWTOP YET?
        BNE    SKIPLOOP     ;IF NO, CONTINUE SKIPPING.
```

```
SYOK    CPY   WNDWBOT        ;SEE IF Y>WNDWBOT
        BLT   SYMORE
        BEQ   SYMORE
        JMP   SDONE  ;IF Y>WNDWBOT, WE'RE DONE

SYMORE LDA    WIDTH
        STA   TEMPCNT        ;INIT COUNTER FOR ONE ROW
        LDA   XLOCHI
        CMP   #$FF   ;IS X<0?
        BNE   SXNOTNEG       ;IF NOT, SKIP
        STY   DTEMPY ;OTHERWISE, STORE Y VALUE
        LDA   XLOCLO ;GET THE ABSOLUTE VALUE OF X
        EOR   #$FF   ;  BY USING ABS(X)=EOR(X)+1
        TAY
        INY
        LDA   (XDIVTBL),Y  ;USE XDIVTBL TO SEE HOW MANY
        CLC           ;   BYTES ARE OFFSCREEN LEFT
        ADC   #$02   ;ROUND NUMBER OF BYTES TO
        LSR           ;   NEXT GREATEST EVEN NUMBER
        ASL
        STA   DTEMPX ;RESULT IS BYTES TO SKIP FOR ROW
        CMP   WIDTH  ;COMPUTE MIN(WIDTH,DTEMPX)
        BLT   SCONT
        LDA   WIDTH

SCONT   CLC            ;OTHERWISE, SKIP ENTIRE
        ADC   FRMBASL       ;   ROW AND UPDATE FRAME DATA
        STA   FRMBASL       ;   PTR ACCORDINGLY
        BCC   SNOINC1
        INC   FRMBASH

SNOINC1     LDA   DTEMPX
        CMP   TEMPCNT        ;IS SHAPE TOTALLY OFFSCREEN LEFT?
        BLT   SCONT1 ;IF NOT, SKIP TO DRAW PARTIAL ROW
        JMP   SNEXTY ;JUMP TO NEXT ROW

SCONT1 SEC            ;SUBTRACT NUMBER OF OFFSCREEN
        LDA   TEMPCNT        ;   BYTES FROM NUMBER OF BYTES
        SBC   DTEMPX ;  IN ROW OF SHAPE
        STA   TEMPCNT
        LDA   #0
        JMP   SXCONT ;DONE WITH CASE WHERE X<0

SXNOTNEG    LDA   XDIVTBL        ;IF X>0, GET START BYTE
        STA   TEMPPTR2  ;   FROM XDIVTBL
```

73

```
        LDA     XDIVTBL+1
        STA     TEMPPTR2+1    ;A POINTER TO THE XDIVTBL IS
        LDA     XLOCHI ;  STORED IN TEMPPTR2
        BEQ     SLT256D       ; IF X>255, ADD 1 TO
        INC     TEMPPTR2+1    ; HI PART OF PTR SO WE GET

SLT256D     STY     DTEMPY ;  TO CORRECT XDIV VALE
        LDY     XLOCLO ;NOW THAT PTR IS ESTABLISHED,
        LDA     (TEMPPTR2),Y ;  GET VALUE FOR X/7
        LSR           ;MAKE SURE WE START ON AN EVEN
        ASL           ;  BYTE BY TAKING BYTE/2*2

SXCONT STA     TMPXBYTE     ;STORE STARTING BYTE FOR TRANSFER
SXCOMP LDA     TMPXBYTE     ;SKIP PAST DATA UNTIL X>WNDWLFT
        CMP     LFTXBYTE     ;IS X>WNDWLFT?
        BGE     SXCONT2      ;IF YES, GO DRAW ROW
        INC     FRMBASL      ;OTHERWISE, WE MUST SKIP
        BNE     SLT256E      ;  PAST MORE SHAPTE DATA
        INC     FRMBASH

SLT256E     DEC     TEMPCNT        ;DECREMENT # BYTES LEFT IN
ROW
        BEQ     SNEXTY ;IF CNT=0, DONE WITH THIS ROW
        INC     TMPXBYTE      ;ELSE BRANCH BACK
        BNE     SXCOMP ;  TO SKIP MORE BYTES OF THIS ROW

SXCONT2     LDA     TMPXBYTE
        CMP     RTXBYTE      ;IS X<=WNDWRT
        BEQ     SXCONT3      ;IF SO, BEGIN DRAWING SHAPE
        BGE     SXCONT4      ;IF X>WNDWRT, DONE WITH ROW

SXCONT3     LDY     DTEMPY ;SHAPE BYTE IS WITHIN
        LDA     (YTABL),Y    ;SCREEN WINDOW, SO
        CLC           ;CALCULATE PROPER SCREEN ADDRESS
        ADC     TMPXBYTE
        STA     HGADRLO
        LDA     #$00
        ADC     (YTABH),Y
        ORA     HGRPG ;GET CORRECT HGR PAGE
        STA     HGADRHI       ;NOW HAVE ADDRESS OF SCREEN BYTE
        LDY     #$00
        LDY     #$00
        LDA     (FRMBASL,X)  ;GET SHAPE BYTE

DEORLOC2     EOR     (HGADRLO),Y  ;EOR WITH WHAT'S ON SCREEN
                        74
```

```
        STA    (HGADRLO),Y  ;STORE IT ON SCREEN
        INC    FRMBASL      ;INCREMENT PTR TO SHAPE DATA
        BNE    SLT256F
        INC    FRMBASH

SLT256F        INC    TMPXBYTE
        DEC    TMPCNT
        BNE    SXCONT2      ;BRANCH BACK FOR REST OF ROW

SXCONT4        CLC          ;NO MORE VISIBLE BYTES ON THIS ROW
        LDA    TMPCNT ;SKIP OVER REMAINING
        ADC    FRMBASL      ;SHAPE DATA FOR THIS ROW
        STA    FRMBASL      ;SINCE RIGHT EDGE OF WINDOW
        BCC    SNEXTY ;HAS BEEN REACHED
        INC    FRMBASH

SNEXTY LDY    DTEMPY
        INY                 ;INCREMENT ROW COUNTER
        CPY    BOTTOMY
        BGE    SDONE
        JMP    SYOK   ;AND DRAW REMAINING ROWS

DONE    RTS

TEMPCNT        DS    1
TXLO    DS    1
TMPXBYTE       DS    1
```

Reader Exercises

I've provided no demo programs this time, since we have merely
enhanced the DRAW routine. You should experiment some more with
the demo program presented last time and make sure that the block
shape clipping works as advertised.

Try animating your object keeping Y constant and varying X from -32
($FFEO) to 320 ($0140). Then try keeping X constant and varying Y
from -16 ($FO) to 191 ($BF). Finally, experiment with CHGUPLFT and
CHGLOWRT to set different graphics windows. Use HLINE to outline
the defined window. Keep in mind that the boundaries of the graphics
window will be on byte boundaries. Use DRAW and XDRAW to

animate objects within the graphics window and clip them when necessary.

You now have most of what you need to design your own animation applications. There are many potential places for improvements in the routines I've presented, particularly in these last two chapters. Depending on your needs, you can write similar routines that run faster for special cases or handle an even more general class of shapes or take up less space. Or you can leave the routines as they are and begin to develop some meaningful graphics applications.

There is still more ground to be covered. Next time we'll look at an application program that demonstrates the smoothest animation possible on the Apple II. Later, we'll talk about another useful type of shape. After that, who knows? You'll just have to stick around to find out!

CHAPTER 8

We're going to discuss the causes of the "tearing" that sometimes occurs when shapes are moved about on the Apple's hi-res graphics screen. Smoother animation can be achieved by using both of the Apple's hi-res graphics screens and a graphics technique called double-buffering.

Flicker

The human eye is very good at certain things and not so good at other things. For instance, it has been shown that the eye can distinguish over 50,000 different colors. It can distinguish somewhere between 32 and 64 intensities of a particular color when two samples are presented separated by some distance. Yet when the two samples are presented side-by-side, a significantly greater number of intensities can be distinguished.

Understanding how the eye perceives color and motion is as fundamental for computer graphics designers as it is for movie-makers and magicians. Flicker is a problem that others have already encountered and studied in some great detail.

Early researchers found that if images were projected fast enough, the eye could be fooled into believing it was seeing continuous motion. Yet, if the speed of projection dropped below a certain threshold, an annoying phenomenon known as "flicker" was detected. The threshold at which flicker can be detected is around 40 frames/second, but differs slightly from person to person.

To overcome this problem, moviemakers made films that were projected at the rate of 48 frames per second. There were only 24 unique frames per second, so each frame needed to be projected twice. Most movies are still projected in this fashion today.

Television was faced with the same problem, and since the bandwidth of video signals is so great, developers wanted to keep the number of frames per second as small as possible without introducing annoying flicker. They settled on a standard of transmitting 30 frames per second. Why then don't TV programs flicker annoyingly? It's because the images are transmitted in an "interlaced" fashion. During the first 1/60th of a second, all the even scan-lines are transmitted, then all the odd scan-lines. This interlacing prevents flicker from becoming objectionable even though only 30 frames per second are transmitted.

Nowadays, more and more graphics systems take advantage of 60 Hertz noninterlaced monitors, which refresh the image 60 times a second without interlacing.

You should be able to imagine what happens if you try to draw a shape as the screen is being refreshed. The graphics memory is being scanned and used to produce a video signal which is sent to the display device. This "refresh" of the video signal happens 30 times a second. If you happen to be modifying graphics memory while this refresh is occurring, you may have only a portion of your change take effect during the current scan. This can happen regardless of how fast you are drawing a shape.

Hopefully, the shape will be entirely drawn in memory by the time the next refresh occurs. If the shape stays in one place, you probably won't even notice that it took two frame times for your shape to appear. However, if the shape is being animated fairly rapidly (say, more than 60 times a second) chances are you'll see a few partially-drawn versions of the shape (tears) as it moves across the screen.

This problem can be avoided entirely by never modifying memory while it's being scanned to generate the video signal. This can be accomplished easily using a graphics technique called double-buffering.

Double Buffering

In graphics, double-buffering means using two graphics buffers to construct images. A static image is displayed, and a second, non-displayed area of memory is used to construct a second image. At a suitable instant of time (during horizontal retrace for instance) the source for the video signal can be switched to the second bank of memory. Nothing gets modified while being scanned out to the video, so there are no tears or flashes. Now the first image can be modified while the second image becomes the static, displayed image.

This can be accomplished on the Apple II using the two hi-res graphics screens. The soft switches $C054 (page 1) and $C055 (page

2) select which of the hi-res graphics pages is being displayed. The location $E6 (which we've called HGRPG) is used to determine the base address of the graphics page which is to be modified. If it contains a $20, graphics are drawn in page I memory. If it contains a $40, graphics are drawn in page 2 memory. By properly setting the switches and the HGRPG location, it is easy to display page 2 while modifying page I and vice versa.

Demo Program

Listing 8.1 contains a short assembly language program that demonstrates this technique. You'll need to load all of the other hi-res subroutines we've developed so far, plus the YTABLE and the sample shape program we developed (or one of your own).

Once again, the YTABLE location is assumed to be $1B00 and the shape table location is assumed to be $8800. (If you use different locations, you'll need to change lines 18, 19, 23, and 25 of the demo program.)

The program starts by initializing the graphics subroutines and clearing both hi-res graphics pages. At line 34, we start the main loop. Shape number I in our table will be animated from x=-64 to x=286, keeping y constant at 64.

During stage one of the loop, we'll display page 2 (line 34) and draw on page I (lines 35-36). Our subroutine to erase the shape from it's old position and draw it in it's new position is contained in lines 58-76. It's the same way we did things last time, with slightly more bookkeeping, since we have to remember that our shape is in different positions on the two graphics screens.

After drawing the shape and pausing to slow down the motion of the shape (line 38 and lines 77-83), we test x to see whether or not we're done (lines 3944). If we have more to do, we'll swap by displaying the newly-modified page I, and erase/draw the shape again on page 2. This process continues until the shape has been moved all the way across the screen. The result is smooth, flicker-free movement of the shape across the screen.

Listing 8.1 - Double Buffering

```
*
* TITLE:    LISTING 1
* FUNCTION: DEMONSTRATE APPLE I DOUBLE BUFFERING
* AUTHOR:   RANDI J. ROST
*
        ORG    $6000
HGR     EQU    $865
HGR2    EQU    $85E
XDRAW   EQU    $B1F
INIT    EQU    $803
SHPTABL        EQU    $FA
SHPNO   EQU    $9
HGRPG   EQU    $E6
DISPPG1        EQU    $C054
DISPPG2        EQU    $C055
PAGE1   EQU    $20
PAGE2   EQU    $40


START   LDX    #$00   ;LOAD ADDRESS OF YTABLE
        LDA    #$1B
JSR     INIT   ;INITIALIZE HI-RES GRAPHICS SUBS
JSR     HGR2   ;CLEAR AND DISPLAY HI-RES PAGE 2
JSR     HGR    ;CLEAR AND DISPLAY HI-RES PAGE 1
        LDA    #$00   ;LOAD POINTER TO SHAPE TABLE
        STA    SHPTABL
        LDA    #$88
        STA    SHPTABL+1
        LDA    #$01   ;DRAW USING SHAPE #1
        STA    SHPNO
        LDA    #$FF   ;START DRAWING SHAPE AT X:-64
        STA    TEMPX+1
        LDX    #$CO
        STX    TEMPX
        LDY    #$40   ;ALWAYS USE Y:64
LOOP1   LDA    DISPPG2        ;DISPLAY HI-RES PAGE 2
        LDA    #PAGE1 ;SET DRAWING TO OCCUR ON PAGE1
        STA    HGRPG
        JSR    SUB1   ;BRANCH TO ROUTINE TO DRAW SHAPE
        JSR    DELAY  ;PAUSE
        LDA    TEMPX  ;SEE IF WE'VE REACHED RIGHT EDGE
        CMP    #$1E
        BNE SCREEN2
```

80

```
          LDA     TEMPX+1
          CMP     #$01
          BNE     SCREEN2
          RTS              ;IF SO, WE'RE DONE!
SCREEN2        LDA     DISPPG1        ;DISPLAY HI-RES PAGE 1
          LDA     #PAGE2 ;SET DRAWING TO OCCUR ON PAGE2
          STA     HGRPG
          JSR     SUB1    ;BRANCH TO ROUTINE TO DRAW SHAPE
          JSR     DELAY ;PAUSE
          LDA     TEMPX ;SEE IF WE'VE REACHED RIGHT EDGE
          CMP     #$1E
          BNE     LOOP1
          LDA     TEMPX+1
          CMP     #$01
          BNE     LOOP1
          RTS              ;IF SO, WE'RE DONE!


SUB1    LDA     TEMPX+1          ;LOAD X POSITION
          LDX     TEMPX
          BNE     TCONT1 ;SUBTRACT TWO FROM CURRENT X SO
          TAY              ;WE CAN ERASE SHAPE AT PREVIOUS
          DEY              ;POSITION TVA
TCONT1 LDY     #$40    ;LOAD V-POSITION (ALWAYS = 64)
          DEX
          DEX
          JSR     XDRAW ;DRAW SHAPE TO ERASE IT
          INC     TEMPX ;ADD 2 TO GET NEW SHAPE POSITION
          INC     TEMPX
          BNE     LT256
          INC     TEMPX+1


LT256 LDX     TEMPX ;LOAD X POSITION
          LDA     TEMPX+1
          LDY     #$40    ;LOAD Y POSITION (ALWAYS = 64)
          JSR     XDRAW ;DRAW SHAPE IN NEW LOCATION
          RTS              ;DONE!


DELAY LDX     #$40    ;DELAY LOOP TO SLOW DOWN MOTION
DELAY2 LDY     #$10
DELAY3 DEY
          BNE DELAY3
          DEX
          BNE     DELAY2
          RTS
TEMPX DS      2
```

Conclusion

Double-buffering is a powerful technique that is available in many flavors on many systems besides the Apple II. It eliminates annoying problems with flicker and image modification by performing modification in non-displayed memory while displaying a static, flicker-free image.

Its chief disadvantages include the amount of memory it takes (two full graphics screens = 16K on the Apple II) and the fact that bookkeeping is made more difficult since shapes can be in different places on the two screens. Nevertheless, if you want extremely smooth motion and can spare the memory, it's certainly the way to go.

In the last chapter, we'll conclude machine language graphics by looking at a slightly different type of shape that we can put to good use. At that time, you should have many of the tools that you need to create superb animation-quality graphics on the Apple II.

CHAPTER 9

In past chapters, we laid the groundwork for doing sophisticated high-resolution graphics and examined routines to clear the screen, draw lines, perform color complements, and create and animate block shapes. Last time we figured out how to do extremely smooth animation using double-buffering.

In this last chapter, we'll look at another type of block shape. By a little careful coding, we'll be able to utilize some of the code that was developed to support block shape animation. We'll make some changes to the shape table generation program we looked at in Chapter 5 to aid in the creation of this new type of shape.

Non-Animation Shape Tables

So far we have developed support for block shapes that were intended to be moved around quite rapidly on the screen. We discovered that the quirks of the Apple's graphics architecture forced us to develop rather lengthy shape tables, with seven frames per shape, to facilitate smooth animation.

Yet, it seems that there exists a large class of shapes that will remain relatively static. One good example is text. Sometimes letters are required to present information (such as a game score). It's not necessary to move these letters smoothly around the screen, so including them in an animation shape table (with seven frames per shape) would be a waste of space. The answer for such "non-animation shapes" is a block shape table that has just one frame per shape. Each shape will be required to start on a byte boundary on the hi-res graphics screen.

Creating Non-Animation Shapes

If you dig out the MAT (Make Animation Tables) program from Part 5, we'll make some modifications to it so that it can be used to create non-animation shapes.

Listing 9.1 shows the changes you need to make to your version of the MAT program to create a program to make non-animation shape tables. After loading in the MAT program replace lines 186 and 210 with the lines shown. (This fixes a bug in the MAT program that caused screen memory addresses to be calculated incorrectly for the bottom two-thirds of the screen.) Save the modified program back onto disk as MAT. Then delete lines 90, 540, 1025, 5000, 5010-5300, and 8080-8400. After typing in the remainder of the lines shown in Listing 1, save the program to disk as MNAT, for Make Non-Animation Tables.

When you run this program, the first four options will function the same as for MAT. You can load in a hi-res screen, adjust the cursor positions, save the table, or generate a single, non-animation block shape. Since these shapes are not shifted at all, there is no need to leave two bytes of space to the right of each shape. The block defined by the cursor is exactly the block that will make up the shape. As in the other program, position the brackets to the top and bottom lines that you want to appear in the shape.

Option #5 allows you to define a bunch of shapes at once. For instance, you can use the DOS Toolkit to draw the letters A-Z on the hi-res screen in a special font. Then use option #5 after positioning the brackets at the upper left of the 'A' and the lower right of the 'Z'. You'll have to specify that the first shape will be shape #65 and that each shape is seven pixels wide. Easy as pie, you have defined shapes 65-90 of your shape table!

We have created the full listing in the Appendix and on the disk image for you if you do not want to type it in yourself.

Listing 9.1 - MAT Program Changes

```
90 REM MAKE NON-ANIMATION TABLES
186 T3=TO- INT(TO/8) * 8
210 Y(I) =8192 + T1 * 1024 + T3 * 128 + T2 * 40
540 POKE START + 2,NUM
1025 PRINT "5) GENERATE SEVERAL SHAPES AT ONCE"
5000 REM ••••• GENERATE SEVERAL SHAPES •••••
5010 INPUT "WHAT NUMBER SHAPE WILL THE FIRST BE?";TS
5015 HOME: VTAB 22
```

```
5020 PRINT "WIDTH OF SHAPES IN PIXELS (MUST BE A": INPUT
"MULTIPLE OF 7)?";WIDTH
5030 WIDTH= INT((WIDTH-1)/7)+1
5040 T3 = INT ((X2 - X1) / (WIDTH * 7))
5050 FOR T4 = TS TO TS + T3
5060 SN =T4
5070 A1 =START + SN • 2 + 1
5080 T1 = PEEK (A1):T2 = PEEK (A1 + 1)
5090 IF T1 =0 AND T2 =0 THEN 5110
5100 PRINT "SHAPE #";SN;" ALREADY DEFINED.....: GOTO 5150
5110 T = AVAIL - A1
5120 POKE A1,T- INT(T/256)*256:POKE A1 +1,INT(T/256)
5130 POKE AVAIL,WIDTH
5140 GOSUB 10000
5150 X1 = X1 + WIDTH * 7
5160 NEXT T4
5170 RETURN
8080 WIDTH = INT ((X2 - X1) / 7) + 1: POKE AVAIL,WIDTH
8090 GOSUB 10000
8100 RETURN
10000 HEIGHT = Y2 - Y1 + 1: POKE AVAIL + 1,HEIGHT
10010 AVAIL = AVAIL +2
10020 FOR I = Y1 TO Y1 + HEIGHT - 1
10030 FOR J = INT(X1/7) TO INT(X1/7) + WIDTH - 1
10040 T = PEEK (Y(I) + J)
10050 POKE AVAIL,T
10060 AVAIL = AVAIL + 1
10070 NEXT J,I
10080 RETURN
```

A Sample Shape Table

Take a look at Listing 9.2. This is a hex dump of a non-animation
shape table that contains definitions for the letters A-I.

The first two bytes of the shape table again provide an offset to the
first byte beyond the end of the current shape table (in case we later
choose to add more shapes to the table.) The third byte indicates the
maximum number of shapes in the shape table. In this case there can
be up to 73 ($49) shapes in the table. (Also recall that for animation
shape tables, the high bit of this byte was set (I). In this case, it's not
set (0). This can be used to identify which shape tables are animation
shape tables and which are non-animation.)

Following this, we again have two-byte offsets for each of the 73 shapes allowed in the shape table. Only shapes 65-73 have been defined for this shape table. Shape #65 is 'A', and the offset is 18 ($12). Adding this to the address of the offset gives us the pointer to the data for the 'A' shape. The address of the offset ($6083) plus the offset itself ($12) gives us a pointer to the shape data ($6095).

The shape data for the letter 'A' begins with the width of the shape in bytes (at $6095), the height of the shape in pixels ($6096), followed by the shape data ($6097-$6090). As you can see, non-animation shape tables are a little more straightforward than animation tables! We have defined each of our letter shapes with its shape number equal to its ASCII value for good reason, as we'll soon see.

If you want, you can type in the hex dump of Listing 2, and type BSAVE LETTER SHAPES, A$6000, L$E8 to save it to disk. Otherwise, take a short timeout now and create your own shape table of letters to use with this demo program.

Listing 9.2 - Non-Animation Shape Table Hex

```
* 6000.60E7

6000:E6 00 49 00 00 00 00 00
6008:00 00 00 00 00 00 00 00
6010:00 00 00 00 00 00 00 00
6018:00 00 00 00 00 00 00 00
6020:00 00 00 00 00 00 00 00
6028:00 00 00 00 00 00 00 00
6030:00 00 00 00 00 00 00 00
6038:00 00 00 00 00 00 00 00
6040:00 00 00 00 00 00 00 00
6048:00 00 00 00 00 00 00 00
6050:00 00 00 00 00 00 00 00
6058:00 00 00 00 00 00 00 00
6060:00 00 00 00 00 00 00 00
6068:00 00 00 00 00 00 00 00
6070:00 00 00 00 00 00 00 00
6078:00 00 00 00 00 00 00 00
6080:00 00 00 12 00 19 00 20
6088:00 27 00 2E 00 35 00 3C
6090:00 43 00 4A 00 01 07 1E
```

```
6098:3F 33 3F 3F 33 33 01 07
60A0:1F 3F 33 1F 33 3F 1F 01
60A8:07 1E 3F 33 03 33 3F 1E
60B0:01 07 1F 3F 33 33 33 3F
60B8:1F 01 07 3F 3F 03 1F 03
60C0:3F 3F 01 07 3F 3F 03 1F
60C8:1F 03 03 01 07 1E 3F 03
60D0:3B 33 3F 33 33 01 07 3F
60D8:33 3F 3F 33 33 01 07 3F
60E0:3F 0C 0C 0C 3F 3F 00 00
```

New Routines

What a bonus! You lucky guys and gals get three new graphics routines to add to your collection! The first two routines draw non-animation shapes In much the same way that ORAWand XDRAWallow you to draw animation shapes. The BLKORAW entry point allows you to overwrite the background with the non-animation shape data, and the BLKXORAW entry point allows you to exclusive-or the shape data with the background.

The BLKDRAW/BLKXDRAW routine is pretty simple. Lines 40-58 (Listing 9.3) compute a pointer to the shape data from the shape number, the start of the shape table, and the offset for the desired shape. The WIDTH and HEIGHT parameters are read from the shape data and stored into locations for later use. The starting byte within the row is computed and stored in XBYTE. By jumping to ORAWSHP in the ORAW/ XORAW routine (didja wonder what that unreferenced label was for?) we can draw our shape!

The PRNTMSG routine is useful for a particular type of non-animation shape table: character sets. PRNTMSG expects to have a pointer to a character string passed in A and X, width of characters in pixels passed in Y, and the location on the screen at which to begin drawing in $06-$08. The last character of the string should have its high bit set so PRNTMSG knows when it's reached the end of the string.

Lines 110-121 of Listing 9.3 define a simple loop which goes through the string a character at a time and calls PDRAW (which just calls BLKDRAW) for each character in the string.

Interestingly enough (you knew this was coming, right?), if our shape table has letters whose shape number corresponds to their ASCII value, we can quickly buzz through the string and pass the letter's ASCII value as the shape number to BLKDRAW. The last character is treated a little differently, since it is necessary to clear the high bit to arrive at a valid shape number.

These routines are actually a lot more flexible than I've indicated thus far. The main limitation is that shapes drawn by these routines must be drawn on a byte boundary. However, that doesn't prevent you from doing your own shifting to define several shapes (some shifted) to use in an animation sequence. Some objects, such as missiles, might need to move as rapidly as seven pixels per jump. If that's the case, they can be designed as "non-animation" shapes. This type of shape also works as well as animation shapes for objects that only move vertically (why?) and it takes up just 1/7 the space. I also suspect some very interesting and powerful "character shape" animation can be done using the PRNTMSG routine. Of course, the shapes need not even be characters! Let your imagination loose and see what kind of creative things you can do with these routines.

Listing 9-3 - Block Shape Draw

```
* THE BLOCK SHAPE DRAW ROUTINES WILL DRAW
* THE SHAPE NUMBER CONTAINED IN $09 AT
* COORDINATES X,Y ON THE HI-RES SCREEN.
* Y SHOULD BE PASSED IN THE Y REGISTER, XHI
* IN A AND XLO IN X.


          ORG     $0DB7
XLOCLO EQU     $06
XLOCHI EQU     $07
YLOC    EQU     $08
SHPNO  EQU     $09
BLKTABL        EQU     $E5
SEQBASL        EQU     $D4
SEQBASH        EQU     $D5
XDIVTBL        EQU     $4C
TEMPPTR2       EQU     $D2
XBYTE  EQU     $0AFE
HEIGHT EQU     $0B00
WIDTH   EQU     $0B01
STOREREG       EQU     $0B05
DEORLOC        EQU     $0C44
```

```
DEORLOC2     EQU    $008C
DRAWSHP      EQU    $0C1A
TEMPCNT      DS     1

BLKDRW JSR   STOREREG        ;SAVE REGISTERS FOR LATER USE
       LDA   #$EA
       STA   DEORLOC        ;STORE NOPS IF
       STA   DEORLOC+1      ;DRAW ENTRY PT USED
       STA   DEORLOC2
       STA   DEORLOC2+1
       BMI   DBLKST
BLKXDRW      JSR    STOREREG
       LDA   #$51
       STA   DEORLOC        ;STORE EOR IF XDRAW
       STA   DEORLOC2       ;ENTRY PT IS USED
       LDA   #$1E
       STA   DEORLOC+1
       STA   DEORLOC2+1
DBLKST LDA   SHPNO ;LOAD SHAPE #
       ASL          ;MULTIPLY BY 2
       TAY          ;STORE RESULT IN Y
       INY          ;ADD 1
       TYA
       CLC
       ADC   (BLKTABL),Y ;ADD OFFSET FOR SHAPE
       STA   SEQBASL        ;STORE RESULTING PTA TO SHAPE
       INY
       LDA   (BLKTABL),Y ;COMPUTE HI BYTE OF
       ADC   BLKTABL+1
       STA   SEQBASH        ;...AND STORE THE RESULT
       CLC
       LDA   SEQBASL
       ADC   BLKTABL        ;ADD SHAPE OFFSET TO
       STA   SEQBASL        ;STARTING ADDRESS OF SHAPE
       LDA   #$00   ;TABLE TO GET FINAL
       ADC   SEQBASH        ;POINTER TO SHAPE
       STA   SEQBASH
       LDY   #$00
       LDA   (SEQBASL),Y ;GET SHAPE WIDTH FROM TABLE
       STA   WIDTH
       INY
       LDA   (SEQBASL),Y
       STA   HEIGHT ;GET SHAPE HEIGHT FROM TABLE
       CLC
       LDA   SEQBASL
```

89

```
        ADC     #$02    ;INCREMENT PTRS TO
        STA     SEQBASL         ;POINT AT START
        LDA     #$00    ;OF SHAPE TO BE DRAWN
        ADC     SEQBASH
        STA     SEQBASH
        LDA     XDIVTBL
        STA     TEMPPTR2        ;GET PTRS TO X/7 TABLE
        LDA     XDIVTBL+1
        STA     TEMPPTR2+1
        LDA     XLOCHI ;IF X>255
        BEQ     LT256A7         ;INCREMENT TEMPPTR
        INC     TEMPPTR2+ 1
LT256A7         LDY     XLOCLO
        LDA     (TEMPPTR2),Y
        STA     XBYTE
        JMP     DRAWSHP         ;DRAW THE SHAPE
```

```
* PRNTMSG CAN BE USED TO DISPLAY A MESSAGE USING THE
* NON-ANIMATION (CHARACTER SET) SHAPE TABLE
* CURRENTLY  IN MEMORY.  THE ADDRESS OF THE MESSAGE
* SHOULD BE PASSED WITH HI BYTE IN A AND LO BYTE IN X.
* THE MESSAGE SHOULD BE A SERIES OF CHARACTER
* BYTESWITH HI BIT OFF, EXCEPT FOR THE LAST CHARACTER
* BYTE, WHICH SHOULD HAVE THE HI BIT SET. THE WIDTH 0
* THE SHAPES IN PIXELS SHOULD BE PASSED IN THE Y
* REGISTER. THE COORDINATE OF THE UPPER LEFT CORNER
* OF THE MESSAGE SHOULD BE PASSED IN THE LOCATIONS          * $
06-$08 WITH $06:XLO, $07:XHI, $08:Y.
```

```
MSGPTR EQU     $FC
PTMPX  DS      2
PTMPY  DS      1
PWIDTH DS      1
PRNTMSG         STA     MSGPTR+1
        STX     MSGPTR ;STORE PTR TO MESSAGE
        STY     PWIDTH ;STORE WIDTH OF CHARS
        LDA     XLOCLO
        STA     PTMPX
        LDA     XLOCHI
        STA     PTMPX+1         ;STORE COORDINATES
        LDA     YLOC    ;OF UPPER LEFT CORNER
        STA     PTMPY   ;WHERE MSG WILL BE
        LDY     #$00
        STY     TEMPCNT         ;ZERO Y INDEX VALUE
PLOOP   LDY     TEMPCNT
```

90

```
        LDA     (MSGPTR),Y    ;LOAD NEXT CHAR OF MSG
        BMI     PDONE  ;IF MSB SET, T'S LAST CHAR
        JSR     PDRAW  ;ELSE DRAW CHAR
        CLC
        LDA     PTMPX  ;ADD WIDTH TO XPOS TO GET NEXT X
        ADC     PWIDTH
        STA     PTMPX
        BCC     PNOCAR
        INC     TMPX+1
PNOCAR  INC     TEMPCNT
        BNE     PLOOP  ;GO BACK FOR MORE CHARS

PDONE   AND     #$7F   ;MASK OUT MSB OF BYTE
        JSR     PDRAW  ;DRAW THE LAST CHAR
RTS
PDRAW   STA     SHPNO  ;ROUTINE TO
        LDA     PTMPX+1        ;LOAD X-Y COORDINATES
        LDX     PTMPX
        LDY     PTMPY
        JSR     BLKDRW ;JUMP TO BLOCK DRAW ROUTINE
        RTS
```

For Example

Listing 9.4 demo program is fairly short. I just wanted to give you an idea of how easy it is to print messages on the screen with your character set font and an assembler. The DCI string directive will define the bytes of data to represent a string with the high bit of the last byte automatically set. Then it's a simple matter to load up the arguments to indicate the string placement and call the PRNTMSG routine and display the strings on the hi-res screen.

To use this program, type it in as shown and save it to disk. Then BLOAD all the routines we've developed in Parts 1-8, plus the routine in Listing 9.3. BLOAD your character set table (or the one in Listing 2) at $8700.

Then BRUN the demo program. You should see the strings "ABCDEFGHI", "DEADHEAD", and "IHGFEDCBA" drawn about in the center of the screen.

Listing 9.4 - Print Message Demo

```
*LISTING 4
*FUNCTION: TEST PRINT MESSAGE ROUTINE
*AUTHOR: RANDI J. ROST
*
        ORG     $6000
INIT    EQU     $803
PRNTMSG         EQU     $E33
HGR     EQU     $865
XLOCLO EQU      $06
XLOCHI EQU      $07
YLOC    EQU     $08
BLKTABL         EQU     $E8
DEMO9   LDA     #$1B    ;LOAD A WITH YTABLE ADR HI
        LDX     #$00    ;LOAD X WITH YTABLE ADR LO
        JSR     INIT    ;SET UP LOOKUP TABLE PTRS
        LDA     #$00    ;LOAD PTR TO SHAPE TABLE AT $8700
        STA     BLKTABL
        LDA     #$87
        STA     BLKTABL+1
        JSR     HGR     ;ENABLE HI-RES GRAPHICS PAGE #1
        LDA     #$40    ;DISPLAY MESSAGE 1 AT (64,64)
        STA     XLOCLO
        STA     YLDC
        LDA     #$00
        STA     XLOCHI
        LDA     #>MSG1 ;LOAD POINTER TO MSG1
        LDX     #<MSG1
        LDY     #$07    ;LOAD WIDTH OF CHARS IN PIXELS
        JSR     PRNTMSG         ;PRINT THE MESSAGE
        LDA     #$50    ;PRINT MSGK2 AT (80,80)
        STA     XLOCLO
        STA     YLOC
        LDA     #$00
        STA     XLOCHI
        LDA     #>MSG2 ;LOAD POINTER TO MSG2
        LDX     #<MSG2
        LDY     #$07    ;LOAD WIDTH OF CHARS IN PIXELS
        JSR     PRNTMSG         ;PRINT MESSAGE #2"
        LDA     #$60    ;PRINT MSG3 AT(96,96)
        STA     XLOCLO
        STA     YLOC
        LDA     #$00
```

92

```
        STA     XLOCHI
        LDA     #>MSG3 ;LOAD POINTER TO MSG3
        LDX     #<MSG3
        LDY     #$07    ;LOAD WIDTH OF CHARS IN PIXELS
        JSR     PRNTMSG         ;PRINT MESSAGE #3
        RTS
MSG1    DCI     'ABCDEFGHI'
MSG2    DCI     'DEADHEAD'
MSG3    DCI     'IHGFEDCBA'
```

The Last Word

With this chapter, the *Graphics Toolkit* draws to a close. I've shared with you an entire collection of powerful machine language routines that you can put to work for you. Hopefully along the way I've taught you a little more about general graphics concepts, the Apple II's graphics architecture, assembly language programming, and software engineering in general.

You should be able to do some pretty nifty things with all the flexible and efficient routines provided. Best of all, you should have learned enough to develop your own routines to provide additional functionality. Hope you've all enjoyed it. I sure have. Happy gaming!

APPENDIX

Make Non-Animation Tables Program

```
90 REM MAKE NON-ANIMATION TABLES
91  REM
92  REM    BY RANDI J. ROST
93  REM         3/30/83
100  REM
101  REM *****   INITIALIZATION   *****
105  DIM Y(192)
110  FOR I = 768 TO 794
120  READ SHAPE: POKE I,SHAPE: NEXT I
130  DATA  2,0,9,0,18,0,26,0,0,45,45,45,222,219
135  DATA  51,54,6,0,63,63,63,76,73,33,36,4,0
140  POKE 232,0: POKE 233,3
150  ROT= 0: SCALE= 1
160  HOME : VTAB 22
170  POKE  - 16297,0: POKE  - 16304,0
175  POKE  - 16301,0: POKE 33,40
180  FOR I = 0 TO 191
185 T0 =  INT (I / 8)
186 T3=T0- INT(T0/8) * 8
190 T1 = I -  INT (I / 8) * 8
200 T2 =  INT (T0 / 8)
210 Y(I) =8192 + T1 * 1024 + T3 * 128 + T2 * 40
220  NEXT I
490  HOME : VTAB 24
500  INPUT "WILL YOU BE USING AN OLD TABLE?";A$
510  IF  LEFT$ (A$,1) = "Y" THEN 700
520 START = 16384
525  HOME : VTAB 24
530  INPUT "INPUT MAX # OF SHAPES FOR TABLE?";NUM
540 POKE START + 2,NUM
550  FOR I = START + 3 TO START + 2 + 2 * NUM: POKE I,0: NEXT
I
560 AVAIL = I: GOTO 900
700  INPUT "TYPE IN NAME OF OLD TABLE?";N$
710  PRINT  CHR$ (4);"BLOAD ";N$
720 START =  PEEK (43634) + 256 *  PEEK (43635)
730 AVAIL =  PEEK (START) + 256 *  PEEK (START + 1) + START
```

```
900  REM *****   MAIN MENU  *****
1000  HOME : VTAB 24
1010  PRINT "1) ADJUST CURSORS  2) GENERATE SHAPE"
1020  PRINT "3) LOAD HGR SCREEN 4) SAVE TABLE"
1025 PRINT "5) GENERATE SEVERAL SHAPES AT ONCE"
1030  INPUT "ENTER WHICH?";A$
1040 T =  VAL (A$)
1045  PRINT
1050  ON T GOSUB 9000,8000,7000,6000,5000
1060  GOTO 1000
5000 REM ••••• GENERATE SEVERAL SHAPES •••••
5010 INPUT "WHAT NUMBER SHAPE WILL THE FIRST BE?";TS
5015 HOME: VTAB 22
5020 PRINT "WIDTH OF SHAPES IN PIXELS (MUST BE A": INPUT
"MULTIPLE OF 7)?";WIDTH
5030 WIDTH= INT((WIDTH-1)/7)+1
5040 T3 = INT ((X2 - X1) / (WIDTH * 7))
5050 FOR T4 = TS TO TS + T3
5060 SN =T4
5070 A1 =START + SN • 2 + 1
5080 T1 = PEEK (A1):T2 = PEEK (A1 + 1)
5090 IF T1 =0 AND T2 =0 THEN 5110
5100 PRINT "SHAPE #";SN;" ALREADY DEFINED.....: GOTO 5150
5110 T = AVAIL - A1
5120 POKE A1,T- INT(T/256)*256:POKE A1 +1,INT(T/256)
5130 POKE AVAIL,WIDTH
5140 GOSUB 10000
5150 X1 = X1 + WIDTH * 7
5160 NEXT T4
5170 RETURN
6000  REM *****   SAVE SHAPE TABLE   *****
6010 T = AVAIL - START
6030  POKE START,T -  INT (T / 256) * 256: POKE START + 1, INT
(T / 256)
6035  HOME : VTAB 22
6040  INPUT "INPUT NAME FOR TABLE?";N$
6050  PRINT  CHR$ (4);"BSAVE ";N$;",A";START;",L";AVAIL -
START + 2
6060  RETURN
7000  REM *****   LOAD HI-RES SCREEN   *****
7005  HOME : VTAB 22
7010  INPUT "INPUT NAME OF SCREEN TO LOAD?";N$
7020  PRINT  CHR$ (4);"BLOAD ";N$;",A$2000"
7030  RETURN
8000  REM *****   GENERATE ENTIRE SHAPE SEQUENCE   *****
```

```
8010  HOME : VTAB 22
8020  INPUT "WHICH SHAPE NUMBER WILL THIS BE?";SN
8030 A1 = START + SN * 2 + 1
8040 T1 =  PEEK (A1):T2 =  PEEK (A1 + 1)
8050  IF T1 <  > 0 OR T2 <  > 0 THEN  PRINT "SHAPE ALREADY
DEFINED...": GOTO 8020
8060 T = AVAIL - A1
8070  POKE A1,T -  INT (T / 256) * 256: POKE A1 + 1, INT (T /
256)
8080 WIDTH = INT ((X2 - X1) / 7) + 1: POKE AVAIL,WIDTH
8090 GOSUB 10000
8100 RETURN
9000  REM *****   ADJUST CURSORS   *****
9010 T = 0: HOME
9011 X1 =  INT ( PDL (0) * 279 / 255):X2 = X1 + 6: IF X2 > 279
THEN X2 = 279
9012 Y1 =  INT ( PDL (1) * 191 / 255):Y2 = Y1
9015 X7 = X1:Y7 = Y1:X8 = X2:Y8 = Y2
9020  XDRAW 1 AT X1,Y1
9030  XDRAW 2 AT X2,Y2
9040  IF  PEEK ( - 16287) > 127 THEN T =  NOT T
9050  IF  PEEK ( - 16286) > 127 THEN T =  NOT T
9060  IF  PEEK ( - 16384) > 127 THEN  POKE  - 16368,0: XDRAW 1
AT X1,Y1: XDRAW 2 AT X2,Y2: RETURN
9070  IF T THEN X4 =  PDL (0):Y4 =  PDL (1)
9080  IF  NOT T THEN X5 =  PDL (0):Y5 =  PDL (1)
9085 X1 =  INT (X4 * 279 / 255):X2 =  INT (X5 * 279 / 255)
9086 Y1 =  INT (Y4 * 191 / 255):Y2 =  INT (Y5 * 191 / 255)
9090 T1$ = " ":T2$ = " "
9100 X1 =  INT (X1 / 7) * 7
9110 X2 =  INT (X2 / 7) * 7 + 6
9112  IF X2 > 279 THEN X2 = 279
9120  VTAB 22: PRINT "X1=";X1;"   ";T1$;: HTAB 15: PRINT
"Y1=";Y1;"    "
9130  PRINT "X2=";X2;"   ";T2$;: HTAB 15: PRINT "Y2=";Y2;"    "
9135  IF X7 <  > X1 OR Y7 <  > Y1 THEN  XDRAW 1 AT X7,Y7:X7 =
X1:Y7 = Y1: XDRAW 1 AT X1,Y1
9140  IF X8 <  > X2 OR Y8 <  > Y2 THEN  XDRAW 2 AT X8,Y8:X8 =
X2:Y8 = Y2: XDRAW 2 AT X2,Y2
9145  GOTO 9040
10000 HEIGHT = Y2 - Y1 + 1: POKE AVAIL + 1,HEIGHT
10010 AVAIL = AVAIL +2
10020 FOR I = Y1 TO Y1 + HEIGHT - 1
10030 FOR J = INT(X1/7) TO INT(X1/7) + WIDTH - 1
10040 T = PEEK (Y(I) + J)
```

97

```
10050 POKE AVAIL,T
10060 AVAIL = AVAIL + 1
10070 NEXT J,I
10080 RETURN
```

www.ingramcontent.com/pod-product-compliance
Lightning Source LLC
Chambersburg PA
CBHW071228170526
45165CB00003B/1038